GENTLEMAN
GEORGE

Gentleman George

George Hardwick

Edited by
John Wilson

Paperback edition published in Great Britain by
Juniper Publishing, Juniper House,
3, Sandy Lane, Melling, Liverpool L31 1EJ
2001

ISBN 0 9528622 8 X

Paperback Edition Typesetting and Origination by:
Norton James Design, Diamond House,
Skippers Lane, Middlesbrough TS6 6PT

Printed and bound by:
Albion Graphics, Old Connelly Complex, Kirkby Bank Road,
Knowsley Industrial Park North, Kirkby, Merseyside L33 7SY

• CONTENTS •

· CONTENTS ·

• Acknowledgements •

To Jennifer Hardwick for her generous
hospitality and total belief in the project.

Research work can often be very time consuming and
I am grateful to the staff of the following local study
departments for their professional assistance :
Middlesbrough, Sunderland, Oldham and Gateshead.

The vast majority of the photographs used in this
publication are from George Hardwick's personal
archive but we would like to thank the following for
their kind permission to reproduce additional material:
Middlesbrough Evening Gazette
and the Oldham Evening Chronicle.

Finally we are deeply indebted to everyone at
Juniper Publishing who worked long sleepless hours
to meet an impossible revised deadline.

J.W.

· A MESSAGE FROM GEORGE HARDWICK ·

In 1998 when John Wilson suggested that I should publish my autobiography I must admit I was very sceptical about the idea. My main concern centred around the prospective market for the rambling reminiscences of an old ex-England football captain who last kicked a ball in anger nearly 50 years ago.

But what a surprise! Two years on, and thousands of hardback copies sold across the country goes to show just how wrong you can be.

Following the many letters and phone calls I've received from well wishers, I would like to thank everyone who has taken the trouble to contact me about the original book. Your kind comments were very much appreciated. In particular I'm pleased that the anecdotes in the text rekindled so many vivid memories of a bygone age, which amazingly, has not only been consigned to another century, but also to the previous millennium.

As a direct consequence of the positive publicity generated by the hardback edition, my life has never been so hectic. Therefore, John and I felt that it would be a worthwhile exercise to update this paperback version of my autobiography with some brand new chapters highlighting my varied experiences over the last two years.

I hope you enjoy reading them.

Kind regards,

George Hardwick

• FOREWORD •

by
Sir Tom Finney

During the Second World War, I spent over three years abroad in the forces. That absence meant George Hardwick and I had never met before my England debut against Northern Ireland, in Belfast, on September 28, 1946.

Sitting in the Windsor Park dressing-room among so many highly regarded players like Frank Swift, Raich Carter, Wilf Mannion and Tommy Lawton, could have been an intimidating experience for me. George, however, understood my apprehension and told me to play my normal game and I would be fine.

His calming influence certainly had the desired effect because I felt totally relaxed during the match, and went on to score my first international goal in our 7-2 victory.

That kind gesture epitomised the thoughtful side of George Hardwick's England captaincy. But, when necessary, he could be a hard taskmaster, particularly if the tide of a game was not running in our favour. George always gave 100% effort, and he demanded the same total commitment from his players.

Everything about George Hardwick's demeanour oozed style. He looked like a debonair matinee idol, with his dark wavy hair and thin moustache. No wonder he was the ladies' favourite.

Once on the pitch, however, he was a classy full-back with a fine left foot, who read the game so well. We pitted our wits against each other on several occasions, both at Deepdale and Ayresome Park, and on the whole I'd say it was honours even.

One of George's finest attributes was that he understood the value of a happy dressing-room and always ensured the England players enjoyed themselves when they were on international duty.

11

Apart from leading his country, he was also the self-appointed social secretary. No matter where we played, at home or abroad, George somehow organised the best tables at restaurants, tickets to the theatre and entrance to the first-rate night spots.

He obviously enjoyed company and had the gift of being able to mix with anybody, whatever their background. That ability made him the perfect choice as England captain.

I was surprised to learn that George had never previously written a book about his varied and interesting life, so it gives me the greatest of pleasure to contribute to his autobiography, which I am sure will be a resounding success.

All the best George.

Tom Finney

• INTRODUCTION •

Football has been George Hardwick's lifeblood. In fact he refers to it as: *A bug without a cure.*

For over half a century George not only played the game at the highest level for Middlesbrough, Chelsea, Oldham Athletic, England and Great Britain, but also coached and managed with great success at home and abroad, and wrote copiously about his passion for football.

No publication could ever hope to encapsulate the diversity and excitement of George's life but, compiled as it is from the many interviews and articles he has recorded and penned over the years, this book attempts to draw together in one informative and revealing volume, how football and "Gentleman George" became and remained inextricably linked.

It was from modest beginnings in a North Yorkshire mining village that George Hardwick's burning ambition to become a professional footballer first took root. Encouraged by his caring parents and close family, he eventually fulfilled that dream and played for his beloved Middlesbrough Football Club.

Then, having overcome a serious career threatening injury sustained in a Second World War bombing raid on his RAF base, George played wartime league football at Chelsea and was selected for England.

After being demobbed, he returned to Middlesbrough and was rewarded with the captaincy of his home town club, followed by the ultimate accolades of leading both England and Great Britain.

Regarded as an excellent coach, George held managerial

positions with Oldham Athletic, the United States 7th Army, the Dutch national team, PSV Eindhoven, Sunderland and Gateshead before developing successful alternative careers in journalism and industry.

To describe George's life as varied and colourful does him a great disservice because if the events were presented as a film script, their authenticity would almost certainly be questioned.

The flickering light of football's golden era is now carried only by two illustrious names: Tom Finney and George Hardwick. The word legend does not do them justice.

John Wilson

Editor

• ONE •

Too big in the backside

As the ball rolled slowly ... so agonisingly slowly ... towards the corner of the net, I knew that goalkeeper Dave Cumming wasn't going to reach it. I just knew it.

All that I could visualize in my mind's eye was the utter despair on the shocked faces of my parents who were sitting watching me from the wooden seats of the North Stand at Ayresome Park. I could see Captain Jack's negative newspaper headlines shouting out from the Evening Gazette's back page: *"Hardwick has nightmare debut"*, *"Manager vows that the teenager will never play again for Middlesbrough Football Club"* and *"Team-mates dumbfounded by schoolboy error."*

I stood still for a second as the ball trickled over the line. I prayed for a gust of wind. Or even a dyed in the wool Red and White Boro supporter racing on to the pitch to boot the ball upfield. But there was nothing to prevent the sickening event taking place. I wanted the hallowed turf to swallow me up and take me well away from the place.

There were more than 21,000 eager spectators in Ayresome Park for the match against Bolton Wanderers and every one of them would believe that I had personally let them all down. They would already have assumed that I was not going to make the grade as a professional footballer. I had failed, at the very beginning of my career.

I felt for a moment as if I was in suspended animation. As if nothing had happened, and I, too, was merely a spectator standing invisible on the pitch. But the realisation sank in fast. I had scored an own goal. AN OWN GOAL! On my Football

League debut. I had dreamed all through Friday night of scoring a goal but at the other end of the pitch. Now I had put the ball past my own goalkeeper. The dream simply turned into a nightmare before my eyes.

I had to quickly pull myself together. I'd been selected for the team on merit and I needed to show the fans that I could play. Besides, there were another 89 minutes to go and we could still win the game.

I was fiercely determined to make amends for my mistake, so I raced into the back of the net, throttled the ball, and launched the ruddy thing as hard as I could towards the halfway line ready for the restart.

I dare say I wasn't the first professional footballer to score an own goal on his debut. I certainly wasn't the last. But I doubt whether anybody has achieved the dubious distinction with their first touch in the opening minute of the match. I never even had the chance to kick the ball cleanly, to pass it, or to make one of my trademark telling tackles. Over the years, I have recounted the story of my own goal many times, always with a broad smile on my face. I can laugh about it now. It happened more than sixty years ago. But it wasn't funny at the time. Not for me, the rest of the team or the 21,000 spectators. I later went on to set many records in my career, but that was the one I wanted least to create.

However, following that inauspicious start, if I'd been told that George Hardwick would later become captain of Middlesbrough, Oldham, England and Great Britain and then manage various clubs and international teams both at home and abroad in a football career which spanned nearly half a century, I would have politely suggested they urgently consulted a psychiatrist, because the notion was too fantastic to even contemplate. Or was it? Despite that early setback, I never lost any of my determination to succeed in the game that I loved. In fact, in some ways it was the catalyst which sent me on the way up the ladder to football success.

If only I could turn back the years and experience every minute of it all again. They were happy days. Immensely happy days. I had a wonderful time growing up, in a loving family, with many good friends around me, in a strong local community. By comparison to the modern era, times were harsh for families in those cash-strapped days of the Depression. But there was an underlying vibrancy, a sense of camaraderie and loyalty which was special, and will live with me forever. I wouldn't have wanted to grow up at any other period in history.

Before I arrived on the scene in February, 1920, my mother, Doris, had been a conscientious primary schoolteacher in North Skelton, near Teesside. My father, Frank, was an electrician working for Pease and Partners, who owned the ironstone mines situated in the nearby village of Lingdale.

During the late Nineteenth Century, the busy mine became the main source of employment in the area. As it developed, it became the lifeblood of a thriving local community, which expanded to around 3,000 residents.

Every day, my father walked the gruelling six miles round trip to work in all weathers from our house in Garnet Street, Saltburn-by-the-Sea. Eventually his journey was made a lot easier when we moved to rented accommodation in the village, on Stanghow Road.

Times were very hard in the 1920s. There was no financial assistance available from any statutory maternity benefit. So, when my mother left teaching in order to look after me, she supplemented our meagre income by scrubbing floors and working in the local newsagent's shop. This was typical of many families in the village at that time. It was hard to make a living, and bring up children at the same time, but there was a strong resolution to get by and make the best of things.

Due to complications with my birth, I was an only child. That led to me developing an extremely close and loving relationship with both my parents. I owe them a massive debt and I can honestly say that I was well and truly cared for.

My father was a jewel of a man who always found the time to support my early passion for football. He was also a very capable sportsman in his own right, playing local cricket for Priestcroft, Lingdale and Saltburn before finally captaining the Smith's Dock team in the West Cleveland League.

He was a chip off the old block and had followed in the athletic footsteps of my grandfather, Francis Hardwick.

Grandad was a well-known figure in the local area, having made appearances for Middlesbrough Ironopolis FC before the turn of the century. He was an excellent and popular all round cricketer playing for, amongst others, Guisborough, Yorkshire Colts, and the Gentlemen of the North. In fact he often played against international touring sides at the annual Scarborough Cricket Festival.

At the time of the festival it was not uncommon to find famous Australian Test players wandering round Lingdale sampling my grandad's generous hospitality at Seaton House, before they also moved on to Stanghow Road.

Occasionally I travelled to Scarborough to watch the cricket matches with grandad in his horse drawn carriage. It was great fun and a marvellous adventure for me. In hindsight I think he would have preferred me to have been a cricketer rather than a footballer. He underlined this fact when he bought me my first cricket bat.

Sport was certainly in the Hardwick genes and I was actively encouraged to participate.

During the school holidays I spent a great deal of leisure time with my grandad and my grandma, who was called Hannah. They kept lots of livestock, including sheep and hens. They also had ponies in a field, and I was allowed to ride them as soon as I was big enough to hold on to the manes. There were no saddles available, so I used to ride the ponies bareback and loved every minute of it.

As a youngster I would often be up at the crack of dawn with grandad to go mushrooming in the local meadows. Sometimes we would walk to the marshes at Charltons to shoot duck, which I would then help him defeather, ready for grandma to cook.

Grandma Hardwick's family had been quite affluent, owning a large tract of land in the Saltburn area. She had been brought up at a place known locally as the White House, and her ancestors had apparently led a colourful past. They were the famous, or infamous, depending on your view of the law, Andrews family, who had earned their clandestine living as smugglers. In order to retain their anonymity, they had excavated a secret tunnel through which to transport their booty from the sea caves in Saltburn cliffs to the White House. Later the labyrinth was extended further, right up to Skelton Castle.

My grandparents' house was situated near a reservoir, the sloping grass banks of which I enjoyed continually running up and down, as kids do. One particular day as I was playing, I noticed that some bees kept flying in and out of the same hole in the bank. Again, as kids do, I grabbed a wooden stick and poked it forcibly into the hole to elicit some reaction.

Almost immediately, the angry residents appeared from the hole and swarmed all over me. In no time at all I was completely covered by the extremely agitated insects. It seemed to me as if there were many hundreds of them. I couldn't even see out of my eyes. It was a nerve racking experience because I knew that I was in serious trouble.

Immediately I ran down the bank in a state of blind panic, calling out as loud as I could: "Grandad, Grandad, Grandad!!!"

When he came out of the house and saw the state I was in, he rushed me to the outdoor tap and dowsed me from head to foot in cold water.

If it hadn't have been for grandad's quick reactions that day, I dread to think of what may have happened to me. The appearance of numerous tender lumps on my body bore testament to my stupidity and was a salutary reminder about leaving bees to their own devices. It was one of my earliest lessons in growing up.

My mother's parents, Alfred and Georgina Moutrey, lived in Saltburn, initially in Garnet Street, before they moved to Marshall Close. During the light summer nights we would often amble from Lingdale through the beautiful local countryside to visit them. It was a pleasant way to take exercise and also develop my keen interest in the local fauna and flora.

Grandad Moutrey was a train driver. He'd followed the trade of his father, who had also worked on the railways. Occasionally he would take me to the sidings where I'd stand on the engine's footplate and help him shovel coal into the burning furnace of the boiler.

The local railway line was adjacent to their house and I remember the thrill of waving to him as his train went rattling by.

Surprisingly, it was to be my Grandma Moutrey who sparked my interest in football when one Christmas she gave me a ball. I was three. I was hooked from the minute that I first kicked that ball. From then on, until I was in my teens, every year there was always a new ball from my grandma. Eventually, to go with the ball, grandad bought me a pair of boots.

Before she was married, Grandma Moutrey was housekeeper to the Bishop of Durham, which in those days was quite a prestigious position to hold. As a character she was what I can only describe as a real lady, and if the truth be known, I was rather in awe of her.

The social skills, table manners, etiquette and respect for others, with which she was so familiar in service, were all shared with me. Those important personal attributes, which say so much about your upbringing, were very useful when I attained positions of responsibility in later life.

In hindsight I was very fortunate to have such close relationships with both sets of grandparents. They filled my life with a rich variety of wonderful experiences and I certainly recognise that their kindness and affection made a very positive, stable and informative contribution to my contented childhood.

Sunday was traditionally the most important day of the week. It was a family day. After attending church in Boosbeck, our relations would often congregate at my grandparents' house in Lingdale for a roast lunch.

In the afternoon a good friend of the family, Reginald "Tim" Williamson, would arrive on his motorbike and sidecar. Tim was the famous international goalkeeper who made a record number of appearances for Middlesbrough. My father then entertained us by singing selections, Mario Lanza style, from his favourite opera The Student Prince, accompanied by my Auntie Dorothy on the piano.

I was surrounded by music at home and although I couldn't play an instrument, I enjoyed absorbing the harmonious atmosphere in the house.

Times were tough during my childhood, but the residents of Lingdale coped well with adversity. Most people kept livestock and many turned their land into miniature market gardens. They grew food and produce, not only for themselves, but also to exchange with their neighbours. Village life had a real sense of community spirit and togetherness. All the kids got on well and although we were always getting into mischief, there was no deliberate vandalism. We respected other people's property.

There were some great characters living in the village. One lady in particular, Dora Carver, was an avid follower of horse racing. I remember after one successful off course bet, which was illegal at that time, she kindly gave my father some money and told him to take me to Ayresome Park to watch Middlesbrough play. It was a wonderfully kind gesture and was typical of the spirit in the village. People often shared what little good fortune they had with others.

As youngsters, I don't think we fully appreciated the depth of the hardship that our parents were living under at the time. Money was very tight, and it was just as well that my mother was very handy with a needle and thread to repair my clothes after the rough and tumble of village and school life.

When I was old enough, I attended the local Lingdale Council School which I enjoyed immensely. Although it was mixed, the girls and boys, whose ages ranged from five to fourteen, were taught in separate classes. On reflection I think it was a good arrangement because you concentrated solely on your work without being distracted by the opposite sex. There was plenty of time to take a keen interest in girls in the future. I like to think that I eventually made up for lost time!

If I was fortunate enough to be allowed my time all over again I would gladly go back to Lingdale School. I was so happy and contented there. The headmaster, Mr Scutt, was an impressive man. Both he and his staff were so committed and diligent that the parents of the village responded to their enthusiasm. I don't think I could have had a better education.

I particularly enjoyed English, maths, geography and music. Our music teacher played us Strauss waltzes and light opera on his turn handle gramophone, and some of those tunes are still among my favourites to this day.

Discipline in school was very strict. Corporal punishment was liberally meted out, either on the hands or the backside, to any miscreants who stepped out of line. During lessons you couldn't turn around to speak to your classmates for fear of receiving a swift clip round the ear to concentrate your mind on the task in hand. It was, however, an environment in which I felt totally safe and secure. Once you understood the ground rules, life was relatively easy to negotiate. I know that many people from my generation look back and say that the discipline did them more good than harm. I totally agree with them.

As far back as I can remember I always wanted to be a footballer. Nothing else really mattered. All the youngsters in Lingdale were crazy about the game. We couldn't fit enough football into the week. At one time or another, grandma's ball and I must have been chased off every field in the village. On clear frosty nights we even played our matches under moonlight. We would have played right through the night if we hadn't been called home to go to bed.

I was a solid lad for my age and began playing for the school team as a junior. I found myself in opposition to boys who were nearly twice my size and age. But I was never intimidated by them. In fact I didn't care how big they were, it simply made me try harder. That was the determined attitude I adopted throughout my career. The tougher the situation I encountered, the more I responded to the challenge.

As a youngster I favoured my left foot so I began my school playing career either out on the left-wing or at centre-forward. Later, in order to become a better all round player, I trained hard and concentrated on improving my right sided technique. The strategy paid dividends because during in my professional career I was equally comfortable in either full-back position or at centre-half.

When I started playing primary league football, all of the players were expected to make their own way to the opposition venue. I was so keen to play at every opportunity that I'd often cadge a free lift to away games from my friend, Peter Twidle, on the crossbar of his pushbike. It was a convenient way to get around. How times have changed. Today even the youngest children are ferried to matches in either cars, people carriers or coaches.

Our matches were played in all weathers and under all conditions. Often in the middle of winter our school pitch in Lingdale would be totally saturated to such an extent that the water and mud covered your boots. The whole pitch was just a morass of mud. Nothing, however, would stop a game of football. We simply played through it.

Most of our school games took place on a Saturday morning and were supported by the whole village. My father even doubled as part-time trainer. He made us run up and down the local shale heaps to improve our fitness levels. Ironically, many years later, I was to buy those same heaps to use as hard core for one of my business interests. Removing the mounds gave me a tremendous amount of satisfaction. I saw it as poetic justice for all the pain they'd inflicted on me in my youth!

All the parents were so involved with the football that I remember the team's woollen socks being knitted by ladies of the local community. The school colours were red and white, which was rather apt as they set a precedent for things to come.

It was not uncommon for between 300 and 400 people to stand on the sidelines and watch a schoolboy match in those days, and during one eventful fixture against Boosbeck I was fortunate enough to score 12 times in a 14-0 win.

Many scouts from professional clubs also attended our games and I vividly recall one particular interested spectator at a match against North Skelton.

During the half-time interval I noticed a rather dapper chappie wearing a bowler hat and carrying a walking stick, talking intently to the headmaster Mr Scutt and my father.

When the game finished, my father called me over to join them. As I stood there, a little bemused and mud-splattered, I distinctly remember Mr Scutt saying: "Anything you discuss with this gentleman will be strictly honourable."

The rotund mystery man turned out to be none other than George Allison, who became the manager of the mighty Arsenal in 1934. He was a local man who, before pursuing a career in journalism, had worked for Middlesbrough FC at the turn of the century in an administrative capacity.

The personal opinion he delivered that morning has been imprinted on my memory ever since, and although I have regaled the story many times over the years, I regularly hark back to it. The statement was profound and to the point.

Allison's overall assessment of my performance concluded that I was a strong player, with a good touch on the ball, who certainly exhibited some potential. He did, however, highlight what he considered to be a physical problem by boldly stating: "You are too big in the backside."

At that young age I was more puzzled than offended by his comment. It just left me wondering why the size of my derriere was so important. It certainly didn't cause me any problems with my football playing!

After the Second World War when I became England captain, I often attended many social functions connected with the national side. At those gatherings I would occasionally meet George Allison. Even then, despite having reached the peak of my professional career, he would still sidle up to me and whisper: "Hardwick, you're still too big in the backside."

Funnily enough, it never did hold me back, though I always had the deepest respect for George. And, despite his comments, I did not become the first person to utter those famous words: "Does my bum look big in these shorts?"

Mr Scutt positively encouraged sport in Lingdale School and it was due to his drive and enthusiasm that our team was very successful in the local schools' football league.

One year we became league champions without dropping a single point, scoring 106 goals against sides representing all the local villages, including Brotton, North Skelton, Boosbeck, Liverton and Loftus.

Knockout competitions were also won. For example, when I was captain in my last season at school, we achieved a notable double, winning the Brotton and Donnison Cups which were then proudly displayed in the school trophy cabinet.

Apart from my father, the biggest influence on my early football career was undoubtedly Mr Scutt and his contribution to the my professional success must not be underestimated. I owe him a great debt.

In the late 1920s my father unfortunately lost his job when Pease and Partners decided that mining the seams of low grade ore was unprofitable.

The closure of the iron workings had devastating consequences on the whole of the Lingdale community and unemployment effected most of the local population. Many people were left with a great deal of unwanted time on their hands and I remember they whiled away the hours playing quoits and using my ball for a kick around in the street.

If times were hard before, they were certainly much worse now, with so many people out of work. It was a difficult period not just for Lingdale, but for the whole country. The Depression of the 1920s and early 1930s affected everybody. But people did tend to stick together and do what they could for each other. Sport, and football in particular, was a welcome distraction from the harsh reality of making ends meet.

Middlesbrough FC, who during the same period were a well-respected and established First Division club, began taking a keen interest in my progress at that time. In fact my parents received a formal visit at our home from two of the club's senior directors, Bill and Bob Rand. It was quite an occasion. The Rand brothers were two of the best known and highly esteemed personalities in North Yorkshire. They carried huge influence both at the football club and in the region. They painted a very rosy picture of life as a footballer and wanted me to sign amateur forms for the Boro. They were educated men, and they made out a very strong case.

However, initially they left empty handed. My mother kept her feet on the ground and informed them that she was worried about the lack of long term career prospects, the possibility of injury, and the overall effect on my education if I signed the forms at that stage of my life. It was a decision which I respected, even though it was the dream of every young lad in the region to play for the Boro, and I was no exception.

Eventually, when I was in my early teens, my mother changed her views and did permit me to sign the forms. It was a big moment in my life and I was able to plan ahead for the future. I was determined to become a professional footballer. However, there were still many bridges to cross. After signing, I was invited to play for South Bank East End Juniors which, to all intents and purposes, was a nursery side for Middlesbrough.

I was so keen to attend the coaching sessions that I walked from my home to South Bank every Tuesday and Thursday after school. It was a long walk, but it meant so much to me. The arrangement, however, was not very satisfactory, particularly on dark winter evenings. So Grandad Hardwick kindly bought me a pushbike on which to cycle the round trip of 14 miles for training. It certainly made things a lot easier.

Many was the time I played two games in a day, firstly in the morning for school and then for East End in the afternoon. I just enjoyed playing in as many matches as I could and thought nothing of it.

The old East End ground, long since gone, had a pronounced slope which fell away to one corner of the pitch. There was also an open space running down one touchline, parallel to the main road. That spare ground was used for training, even though in the middle of winter it often resembled a freezing cold swamp. Being situated next to the main road did have its advantages, as the street lamps cast enough light across the ground for us to spend hours and hours practising our skills in marathon floodlit five-a-side matches.

After training there was always a hot bath waiting for us in the little wooden changing rooms supervised by the two enthusiastic volunteer trainers Jacky Cotterill and George Morris.

My contemporaries in the same East End side included Paddy Nash and Harold Shepherdson, both of whom went on to play professionally at Ayresome Park.

During the Depression, junior football was thriving in the South Bank area with teams representing East End, Princess Street, St Mary's and St Peters. It was a hotbed of football and, while there were often big and enthusiastic crowds to see games in those days, a percentage of the watching fans were actually scouts and representatives from the major clubs.

It was a great learning period for me, playing against lads of similar ability, all of whom had the same aspirations to become professional footballers. For many of us, it was our one big chance of fame, even if professional footballers in those days did not earn a great deal more than many normal workers in industry. We were all determined to prove ourselves and hopefully take that next big step towards winning a contract with one of the top professional clubs.

I hadn't been playing very long at that level before I encountered the talents of a small, skilful, blond haired lad with a fast growing reputation.

When you are a youngster, certain names reverberate around an area like wildfire. It was usually because somebody was handy with their fists and was a must to avoid. The name of Wilfred Mannion, however, was already gaining a degree of notoriety among the ranks of the local junior footballers.

Even in those days it was apparent that Wilf had natural talent to burn. He already possessed lightning control, an outrageous body swerve and cheeky tricks that occasionally got him into trouble for taking the mickey out of the older lads. The game came easily to him, probably too easily.

We both played in many keenly fought local derbies, often in front of crowds in excess of 4,000. As I recall, under my captaincy, East End occasionally came out on top, against St Peters winning the North Riding Junior Cup and the Junior League Challenge Cup.

From the junior ranks I graduated to the East End senior side, playing at either left-back or on the left-wing alongside some great lads including Jack and Percy Kurnow, Sam Mitchell, Hugh Duffy, Jack Trainor, Jackie Blakeman, Frankie Gordon, Ernie Leadstone, Tich Cooper, Sid Appleyard, George Snaith, Micky Parsons and George Turnbull.

It was George who took me under his wing after I'd taken a real pasting in a game against Portrack Shamrocks from Stockton-on-Tees. They were a team which a future colleague and friend of mine, Mick Fenton, used to play for, prior to him signing professional forms for Middlesbrough in 1932.

Mick, over the years, has gained something of a reputation as a great story teller, and recalling the name of Portrack Shamrocks reminds me of a tall tale he used to recount about a very short-sighted player who once turned out for the Stockton side.

During the course of one particular game, and Fenton swears this is true, our myopic friend committed an outrageous foul by deliberately kicking an opposing defender extremely hard up the backside. The poor guy was left prostrate on the ground, writhing in obvious agony. As the referee rushed towards him brandishing his notebook, he indignantly commented to the official that the ball was too soft and needed changing. It was a nice try, but still resulted in a booking.

During a thoroughly enjoyable time with South Bank East End, I captained the junior team to success in the North Riding Junior Cup and in the same season was a member of the senior side which won the North Riding Senior Cup. To cap it all, we also had a good run in the FA Amateur Cup before eventually losing to the mighty Bishop Auckland. They were very happy days indeed.

However, there was no guarantee that I would eventually make the grade as a professional. Even though I was completely dedicated towards trying to take the next step up the ladder with Middlesbrough, I had to accept that the competition was fierce and that many excellent young players who possessed similar talents and dedication as myself would not complete the transition to being professional footballers. I could be one of the unlucky ones who would fail to make it.

So, when I left school at 15 I had to find a job, which might lead to a career outside football. I took employment in the drawing office at Dorman Long's Steelworks near Middlesbrough for 7s 8d a week. It was a good start, and my family was pleased. My mother, for reasons previously stated, wanted me to have a skilled trade to fall back on, and I understood her concern.

By that time we had moved from Lingdale to pleasant rented accommodation in a terraced house in Aire Street, South Bank, where my father had found employment as an electrician at Smith's Dock shipyard on the River Tees. My mother was also working in the local council offices. Our new home was ideal for me because it meant no more long bike journeys. I was practically living next door to the East End ground. Everything was rosy for the Hardwick family, especially as we were all now achieving. It was a very happy time because there was a lot of pressure removed from the family due to the fact that three regular wages were coming into the household.

At the same time, I continued to show promise on the football field and began to play as an amateur for Middlesbrough Reserves. Turning out for the Stiffs, as the second team was affectionately called, was the first real stepping stone on the way to becoming a professional.

On the strength of my consistent performances as an amateur for South Bank East End and Boro Reserves, I was delighted when, at the age of seventeen, I was asked to sign professional forms for Middlesbrough Football Club. I was one of three young lads who were signed by the club on the same day. The others were Jimmy McCabe, again from East End, and George Wardle, of McKay Sports Durham.

My mother, bless her, finally agreed to me signing a full-time contract because she realised that football was THE great passion in my life. It was May, 1937, and a very significant date in the life of George Hardwick.

I had felt for some time that I was going to end up as a professional player. Other First Division clubs, particularly Aston Villa and Birmingham, had also been keen to acquire my signature and there had been discussions with their representatives. However there was only one club I wanted to play for, and that was the Boro.

There was also the important matter of a wage increase. I was paid the princely sum of £6 a week during the season and a £4 retainer for the summer months. That rose to £8 and £6 just before the war, plus bonuses. £2 for a win and £1 a draw. And it goes without saying that you played like hell to ensure you received your supplementary bonus.

In comparison to the huge over-inflated salaries received by today's top Premiership players, my wages now appear to be quite minuscule. But in those days, with so many people out of work, it was a real privilege to play football for a living. Even skilled tradesmen were only earning around £2 10s. Football was a profession which was well respected. The most famous players were lauded, and for me to be given the opportunity to play for my home town club filled me with enormous pride. My contemporaries and I played football because we loved the game. It certainly wasn't for the money.

The North-eastern region was once christened the hotbed of soccer because of the steady stream of outstanding players who came from the coal mining and shipbuilding areas to take up the professional game. Between the wars, like most youngsters from industrial Teesside, I had a great affinity with Middlesbrough FC. They had in their ranks quality internationals including Jackie Carr, Billy Pease, Maurice Webster, Bobby Bruce and the goal machine George Camsell.

Many of the local lads at that time aspired to one day pull on the famous blood-red shirt worn by those star players. I was very fortunate to achieve that ambition. Most, however, were not.

Throughout my career and in fact my life, I made sure that I never forgot where I had come from and who I was. It was very important to constantly remember that I was fortunate to be blessed with a talent, part of which was a natural talent, but most of which had been nurtured in me by the dedication and hard work of many other people. It helped me to keep my feet on the ground throughout my career and ensured that I never lost my hunger to achieve everything that it was possible for me to achieve.

• TWO •

The nakedness of the long distance footballer

I was now a full-time professional footballer with Middlesbrough Football Club and determined to try to make a big impression. I started the 1937/38 pre-season training programme alongside members of the first team, all of whom were household names throughout Teesside. I was in exalted company. I quickly realised, however, that there was strict established pecking order within the club ranks, and a fresh faced new boy like me featured very low down on the list, and probably off it.

As a young professional I was given many menial chores to perform to reinforce my subterranean status, like sweeping out the changing rooms and cleaning the senior players' boots. The latter task I actually enjoyed and made sure that the footwear of the club skipper, Bob Baxter, always received an extra polish. It was an honour to clean the boots of the great man.

Baxter, who was without doubt my favourite Boro player and mentor, had signed for Middlesbrough in rather peculiar circumstances.

In the early 1930s Boro manager Peter McWilliam was on a scouting mission in Scotland and watched the match in which Baxter was playing only by chance because his intended fixture had been postponed. He was impressed with what he saw and offered Baxter the opportunity to move south.

A strange quirk of fate maybe, but during his time at Ayresome Park, Baxter played in almost every position for the club, before eventually settling as a cultured centre-half. He was a very skilful player and would often give the manager and fellow defenders palpitations by deliberately dribbling the ball in and around the penalty area. His actions were a cause of great consternation to goalkeeper Dave Cumming, whose broad Aberdonian shouts of: "Baxter, Baxter, get rid of it, get rid of it!!!!!" became more frantic and hysterical the longer Bob dwelt on the ball. I'm sure he enjoyed teasing poor Dave, because when he eventually cleared the ball, he would laugh out loud at the panic he'd caused.

There was a great team spirit and camaraderie in the Ayresome Park dressing-room with most of the Boro players, such as Billy Forrest, Cumming, Jackie Milne, Mick Fenton and future Scottish captain Baxter all budding comedians with wicked senses of humour. Day after day I went home with my stomach muscles aching from laughing at their slapstick antics.

But joking aside, they could certainly play. Controlling, holding and manoeuvring the ball was second nature to them and I soaked up everything I saw. It was a great learning experience and the start of my professional football education. If I could not learn from such talented players as these, then I would never learn.

As a new professional you had to conform to certain standards imposed by the club. Amongst other things, you were expected to be well groomed, clean shaven, wear a tie and represent the club with a certain amount of decorum on away trips. Failure to comply with the regulations would lead to severe reprimands and in extreme cases you were dropped for the next match. Respect was also given a high priority, with the senior professionals being addressed as Mr Forrest or Mr Baxter.

I remember during one five-a-side game when Bob Baxter called me for a pass. Instead of giving him the ball I feinted to do so, and then shot for goal. I thought I'd done quite well, but all I received was a painful clip round the ear and a stern rebuke to remind me that when the skipper called for the ball he'd better receive it bloody quick. That lecture again cemented my appreciation of the humble standing I held within the club ranks.

The established stars constantly reinforced our subservient existence at Ayresome Park and were unmerciful in the stunts they used to pull on the youngsters. Their favoured pastimes were throwing us fully clothed into a cold bath, hiding our trousers, nailing our shoes to the dressing room floor and placing firecrackers under the treatment table.

They even conned Wilf Mannion on one away trip to London into believing that a reporter from a national newspaper was willing to pay him for an exclusive interview after breakfast in the hotel reception.

By lunchtime, when the rest of the squad returned from their Saturday morning stroll, poor Wilf was still sitting in the foyer keeping his lonely vigil until the disguised voice of Jackie Milne whispered: "This is the Daily Mail. Could I speak to Wilf Mannion please?" At that point the whole playing party burst into roars of laughter and Wilf finally realised he'd been taken for a ride.

There was never any danger of the young professionals becoming conceited, and with tricks like that being played on us you needed to keep your wits about you at all times.

Most of the escapades are unfortunately too lavatorial and vulgar to repeat in the public domain, but anybody who has been in a club dressing-room, at any level of sport, will understand our situation. The following milder examples will give the reader some idea of the constant torment we had to endure, all in the name of our football education.

The club trainer at that particular time was the long-serving Charlie Cole, who was also a very highly respected local athletics coach. One of his favourite core activities in the weekly training programme was long distance running, which was designed to build up our stamina levels. It was, however, an activity which few of the players relished. In fact once we'd left the ground, out of Charlie's view, the senior lads always consciously slowed the pace right down to a very leisurely jog. The youngsters were then threatened, in no uncertain terms, not to overtake them or else.

On one particular wintery morning we were all sent out on to the streets of Middlesbrough for stamina training and as usual the established stars began clowning around at the front of the group. As we jogged along Roman Road, Green Lane and Acklam Road the young lads at the back used the pedestrian pace as an opportunity to pepper the first team with snowballs. Strangely, there was no immediate response.

That lack of instant retaliation should have served as a warning because as we turned the next blind corner into Church Lane we were ambushed by the senior players, who were lying in wait for us. We were grabbed by several pairs of hands and stripped naked. It was impossible to resist. There were at least half a dozen of us subjected to the ignominious ordeal including Wilf Mannion, Harold Shepherdson and myself. It was our punishment for throwing the snowballs. We were left freezing and shivering in the street without so much as a stitch to cover our embarrassment. I can't imagine what passers-by must have thought as we stood there desperately trying to hide our modesty. As the senior players gleefully ran off carrying all our kit, we hastily sought sanctuary in the barn of a local farmhouse, away from public view.

When the first teamers eventually arrived back at Ayresome Park, minus their young companions, Charlie Cole tentatively enquired as to our whereabouts. He was then handed the empty tracksuits in the form of a large clue.

About half an hour later it was a great relief to see Coley cycling up the lane with our gear. But then we had to return to Ayresome Park and endure our assailants jeers of derision before we could thaw out.

Even Charlie Cole wasn't exempt from becoming the butt of the senior players' practical jokes and one aromatic incident springs to mind.

Ralph Birkett, our international right-winger, was a part-time dog breeder. One morning when his wife was unavailable, he had to bring half a dozen pups to training. Charlie Cole was not best pleased with the club's new recruits and insisted they must be housed somewhere safe during training.

When Charlie left us to get changed, Bob Baxter suggested they could easily be accommodated in the small, well heated, but poorly ventilated room used for drying our wet training gear. Ralph was rather sceptical about the idea but as time was pressing, the pups were playfully led to their temporary place of sanctuary.

A few hours later, with training complete, the senior players, unusually for them, didn't linger in the dressing-rooms. They were washed, changed and out of the ground in double quick time.

The reason for their hasty exit soon became apparent. The air was suddenly filled with the bellowing voice of Charlie Cole, who was standing outside the drying room with his hand covering his nose. He'd opened the hothouse door and was greeted by the pungent aroma of au de excrement which was overpowering enough to fell an elephant.

Poor Charlie spent the rest of the afternoon swilling out the drying room floor. But it was some time before that not so fragrant puppy perfume was totally eradicated from his nostrils. Needless to say Ralph Birkett's canine friends were not booked for a return visit to Ayresome Park.

Creating and retaining the right atmosphere is a vital prerequisite for any football club because without harmony in the dressing-room there is simply no team spirit out on the pitch.

In order to achieve that togetherness many of the Boro players, before and after the Second World War, met socially outside the club. They were also involved in the many charity events held at local bowling greens, cricket grounds and golf courses.

Some of the lads were very proficient indeed at other sports. For example Wilf Mannion was a very accomplished billiards player, Ronnie Dicks an excellent bowler, Harry Bell and George Dews were county standard cricketers, while Bob Baxter was a proficient low handicap golfer.

I shall never forget my first introduction to the fairways with dear Charlie Cole during a special training week at Cleveleys Hydro, Blackpool.

By the time we arrived at the course the more competent foursomes had already teed off. They were followed by the youngsters, who were left to hack around with our bowler hatted trainer.

Early in the round I managed to keep the ball moving in the required general direction but didn't manage to win a hole. By the time we reached the fourth tee it was still Charlie's honour to drive off.

The tee was situated on top of a small hillock with the green strategically positioned over the far side of a large pond.

Charlie unfortunately mishit his first shot and Wilf Mannion and I watched as it gently rolled down the slope to be devoured by the waiting water hazard. His second effort followed a similar route and by now his frustration and embarrassment were beginning to grow.

By the time his fourth attempt had also disappeared with an all to familiar sounding plop, Mannion and I were doubled-up, crippled with laughter.

That was the final straw. Charlie completely lost his temper, and after swinging a couple of wide circles around his head to attain the required momentum, the miscreant brassie sailed majestically through the air to join the balls in their watery grave.

Eventually when he'd calmed down, and the red rage had drained from his face, we helped him retrieve the offending club from the pond.

After such an hilarious introduction to the game, who could fail to become hooked. Over the next few months my play improved so much that I was eventually invited to tee off with the competent foursomes.

When I joined Middlesbrough the pipe-smoking Wilf Gillow was the manager. He'd been appointed in 1934 and the club had shown a steady improvement every season under his guidance, reaching a creditable fourth place by 1938/39. He was generally an amiable man but could be hard if the need arose.

Training started at 9:30am on the dot, with a large portion of the time spent jogging aimlessly around Ayresome Park. Many was the time I wished the pitch had been smaller as we completed twelve monotonous circuits in the morning, followed by a similar number in the afternoon.

I have to confess I was not the quickest of players, so full-back Bobby Stuart, who was a virtual flying machine, was detailed to give me extra sprinting practice. I must say he certainly helped me to find another couple of yards of pace which improved my all round game.

We also had no formal training pitch, although after the war we were bussed down to the beach at Saltburn for some coaching sessions. In the winter, that could be a very bracing experience indeed with the penetrating wind whipping into your face off the cold North Sea.

There was very little time allocated to skills practice. To be given a ball was considered a treat in those days and tactical discussions were kept to a minimum. Games were won and lost by the individual ability of the eleven men on the pitch. We always concentrated on our own strengths and were never immersed in the quality of the opposition.

The majority of our shooting and heading practice took place behind Ayresome Park's North Stand, against the surrounding walls or on makeshift head-tennis courts and five-a-side pitches. Today those very basic facilities must sound quite primitive and archaic to the modern footballer and supporter, brought up on multi-million pound soccer academies. Over the years, however, they certainly helped to produce some great Boro players. Just ask any of the supporters from my generation.

The choice of my first pair of professional football boots was done under the watchful eye of Charlie Cole. My initial fitting was done in bare feet. I normally took a size $7^{1}/_{2}$ in a shoe but I was made to squeeze into a size six brown leather boot. They were a hell of tight fit and I could manage only a few minutes at a time with them on. It was a slow painful torture even to walk in them.

Eventually after many hours of breaking them in, they were supple enough to take a thin sock. By the time of the first official practice matches those boots were moulded to my feet and fitted me like a pair of gloves.

I acquitted myself well during the early practice matches and, on the strength of one performance, when I marked England international Ralph Birkett out of the game, I was selected for the second team.

I made my professional debut in the North-Eastern League against a team from Jarrow. Our side contained many players with first team experience, including Scottish international Benny Yorston, who was testing out an injury.

The league had a reputation for producing hard men. It produced lads who certainly had technical ability but were lacking in fitness because of their penchant for supping the local brew to excess. They did, however, enjoy testing themselves against the professionals. They had very little respect for players who enjoyed the luxury of being paid to play the game. The matches were physically very tough indeed, and that's an understatement. But it was great experience and I quickly learned how to look after myself.

I vividly remember the robust nature of my first match and the dulcet tones of an expressive Geordie voice in the crowd, shouting out: "Why ya big dorty bugga, I wish ye wa playin' fa us", as our experienced full-back, Billy Brown, made a very solid but fair challenge on the opposition winger.

One Thursday morning in December, after some steady games for the reserves, I was pleasantly surprised to find my name on the 1st XI's team-sheet pinned to the green baize noticeboard. I'd been chosen to make my debut against one of the league's strongest teams at that time, Wolverhampton Wanderers, when the regular left-back Bob Stuart picked up a long term injury.

My selection, as one of the youngest players to don a Boro first team shirt, was very unexpected. The club had older full-backs on which to call, like Henry Fowler, but obviously they'd decided that I was making enough solid progress to warrant my chance. It was still a magical moment in my career. Once I saw HARDWICK written behind the name of left-half Billy Forrest, I didn't walk home to tell my parents, I simply floated on air.

To play for Middlesbrough was not only a personal achievement but it was also the culmination of the sacrifices made by my parents when, during the hard times of unemployment, they had kept me strong and healthy. I resolved there and then that I would not let them down. I was determined to carve out a footballing career of which they could be justly proud.

Prior to the match, instructions were left with the Wolves groundstaff by their colourful team manager Major Frank Buckley, to prepare a soft surface which he believed would favour the home side. So, on the Friday afternoon, in order to comply with the request, the local fire brigade were summoned to pour gallons of water onto the Molineux ground. Unfortunately nobody had bothered to check the local weather forecast and there was a heavy overnight frost. By Saturday morning the pitch was a rock hard skating rink and, to my disappointment, the match was postponed.

Once we knew the game was off, all the Boro players went to Villa Park to watch Aston Villa beat Sheffield Wednesday. Surprisingly it was the first league game I'd ever watched away from Ayresome Park. In fact I was quite taken aback by the experience, especially as the large partisan Brummie crowd made a tremendous atmosphere.

As an interested observer, what caught me unawares was the speed of the game, particularly when the Villa outside-right Frankie Broome was in possession. It made me realise that I was now expected to play at that level and cope with whatever the opposition could throw at me. And there were many international class right-wingers around at that time, I can tell you. But, even at that young age, I had a great belief in my ability to cope with the challenge and it made me more resolute to do myself justice when the chance next came along.

I eventually made my debut the following week at home to Bolton Wanderers in front of 21,000 fans. I could never have dreamed that I would end up scoring an own goal in the first minute, though I felt that I acquitted myself well over the next 89 minutes and deserved to stay in the side.

As a matter of interest, although I played the majority of my professional games at left-back I always thought the easiest position on the football field was centre-half. And that opinion is not meant to belittle the achievements of the great number fives I've had the privilege of knowing throughout my career. I just felt that playing at the heart of the defence, with the action always in front of you, made the game so much easier to read.

Unlike some players who spend their time pacing up and down the changing room or locked in the bathroom, I never suffered from nerves before a game. In the run up to the match I was positively excited rather than negatively apprehensive about my forthcoming debut.

It probably helped me to cope a lot easier with the fact that I did not make the most auspicious of starts to my first team career.

Straight from the kick-off the ball was moved out to the Bolton left winger Alf Anderson, who quickly ran down the touchline to attack our right-back George Laking.

Anticipating a centre, I positioned myself on the edge our penalty area.

As the expected cross came into the box Bob Baxter and the Bolton centre-forward Jack Milsom both went for the ball but it broke free and came towards me. There should have been no problem. In fact there was no problem. I'd dealt with similar mopping up situations on numerous occasions. The playing surface, however, was a bit icy so I opted for safety first tactics. Without looking, I simply hooked the ball back to our reliable goalkeeper Dave Cumming.

Satisfied I'd carried out my defensive duties proficiently, I was about to make my way towards the halfway line when I heard a loud groan from the crowd.

As I turned round to find out the cause of their negative reaction, I saw Dave frantically slithering across his goal on his hands and knees, and the ball trickling agonizingly into the corner of the net for an own-goal. He was not going to reach the ball and, for a moment, I wanted the ground to swallow me up. I couldn't believe what I'd done on my debut.

Bob Baxter, our captain, came straight over to tell me not to worry and, to be quite honest, I didn't. That unfortunate mishap galvanised me into action and had the affect of making me even more determined to play well and rectify my mistake.

My positive reaction was noted in one of the match reports:

"I wonder what part of the incident is most vivid in his memory. For my part the sight of Hardwick, having stabbed the ball back beyond the reach of his goalkeeper, walking into the net, picking up the ball and punting it down field sticks most. It showed that even in a crushing circumstance like this, the youth was calm and collected and I think his play afterwards confirmed it."

Despite creating a gilt-edged chance for George Camsell, which under normal circumstances he would have drilled in for an equaliser, my efforts came to nought and we eventually lost the match 2-1.

At least I have the consolation that the incident provides me with a vivid and lasting memory of the occasion. Often when you talk to other players they have no recollection of their debut day. It just passed them by. That most certainly did not happen in my case. After that unfortunate first touch, I went on to play in a game which is indelibly stamped on my memory forever.

At the time I believe it may well have been the quickest own goal ever scored by a debutant in the history of league football. I wonder if anybody has since beaten my "achievement".

Despite my error I was given an extended run in the team for a couple of months, because of Bobby Stuart's injury.

During that initial spell I played in my first North-east derby against Sunderland on New Year's Day.

Ayresome Park's impressive new South Stand had recently opened and a pre-war record crowd of almost 46,000 attended the game. That encounter gave me an appetite for the big match atmosphere and it was a desire I would never lose during the whole of my playing career. The more important the occasion, the better I liked it.

The build up to the game was rather emotional because one of the father figures of Middlesbrough Football Club, former chairman Phil Bach, had passed away. In tribute, the players of both sides wore black arm bands and observed a two minute silence in the centre circle.

Sunderland had a great forward line in those days which read: Duns, Carter, Gurney, Gallagher and Connor. But a Boro team including three novice youngsters, Hardwick, Mannion and my old clubmate from South Bank East End Paddy Nash in goal, received rave reviews in a thrilling 2-1 victory. It was an afternoon to savour.

I also made my FA Cup debut in a 2-0 home win over Second Division Stockport County with Mick Fenton scoring both goals. Mick at that time was gaining a national reputation for his power shooting. The dynamite in his boots must have all been down to timing because his shoulders weren't wide enough to wear a pair of braces. He scored around 60 goals in the two seasons prior to the Second World War and gained a much deserved international cap for England, at Wembley, in April 1938. He was some finisher, I can tell you.

The extended run in the first team also saw my first encounter with a certain outside-right called Stanley Matthews, in a mudbath at the Victoria Ground, Stoke. Even in such atrocious conditions The Wizard of the Dribble was quick and nimble on his feet and we eventually lost the match 3-0.

My performance against the maestro was sympathetically treated in the press, who noted:

"The seventeen year old Hardwick was at times sorely troubled by the Matthews magic but stuck to his task manfully and finished the game on level terms with the Stoke star."

I never thought on that rain-sodden day in the Potteries that just three years later I would be lining up with the mercurial Stan in an England shirt. Then, after the Second World War, I'd be captain of my country and he'd be a member of my team.

Watching World Cup 1998 on television, and hearing the players complaining about the lightness of the ball, reminded me of the lead weight we had to play with during that Stoke City game.

Towards the end of the match I unwisely put my head in front of a Freddie Steele piledriver. Where there's no sense there's no feeling. The very heavy wet ball seemed to totally envelop my head like a muddy helmet. Somebody joked that it was only my ears that stopped me from suffocating.

When the final whistle blew, I was led from the field by our trainer Charlie Cole suffering from my first bout of concussion and a neck that felt about two inches shorter. Everybody knows how leaden the balls became in those days when they absorbed the moisture and rapidly increased in weight. You had to be a brave man to head the ball in waterlogged conditions, but most players thought nothing of it. I wonder how many of today's stars would volunteer to head a sodden leather casey from my era when it had been struck with pace and power.

In my opinion the most accomplished game I played during that spell in the first team was away against Chelsea.

Ironically a few years later when I guested for the London club during the war, I learned following that game that the Pensioners had made an unsuccessful attempt to purchase my services from Middlesbrough. It was a fact which my hometown club somehow neglected to tell me.

In the league that season, we mounted a serious championship challenge, but a run of seven matches without a win after Easter saw us settling for fifth spot.

Although I eventually returned to the reserves, when Bobby Stuart was restored to full fitness, my initiation into top flight football had left me confident in my ability. I felt I could hold my own in the First Division.

During the close season I spent the summer playing tennis and cricket. I enjoyed both sports but later had the indignity of being disqualified from a mixed doubles tennis tournament in Redcar because I was classified as a professional sportsman. The enforcement of that peculiar ruling made the organising authorities a laughing stock. Although my game was competent, I was hardly Pete Sampras standard.

I played cricket for Normanby Hall in the North Yorkshire and South Durham League with my dear friend Harold Shepherdson.

As a person Harold was kind, thoughtful and conscientious. A real gentleman in the truest sense of the word. We remained close associates for over half a century. Although he didn't pull up any trees as a player, Harold fully capitalised on the skills he learned as a wartime physical education instructor when, as a trainer, firstly with Middlesbrough and then England, he established a professional reputation which commanded total respect from those who mattered within the game.

One of my lasting memories of him was seeing his reaction to the final whistle at the end of the 1966 World Cup Final at Wembley. Harold, who was sitting on the bench next to the manager, Alf Ramsey, leapt six feet into the air to acclaim England's tremendous victory over West Germany. That display of delight typified the commitment he brought to his work.

Harold also used to derive a good deal of pleasure from recounting a wartime tall tale in which he claimed that the Boro secretary at the time, Herbert Glasper, told Mick Fenton that if he wanted his travelling expenses reimbursed he'd better catch me because I'd already beaten him to all the gate money. Shep always said, even in those days, that I had expensive tastes. He is sadly missed.

After a few games in the Normanby Hall seconds, I was promoted to the first XI. Although never in the same class as my Grandad Hardwick, I was an enthusiastic cricketer and made a few runs as a hard hitting batsman. After the war, my efforts at the crease helped Normanby Hall to win the league championship and the local Kerridge Cup Final.

From a personal point of view, the new season 1938/39, was one of total frustration. After breaking into the side at the age of seventeen I'd expected to be chosen more often for first team duty. Although I frequently travelled to away games as twelfth man, and was included in all the special training sessions, I didn't make a single appearance. I was very disappointed.

For part of that summer Middlesbrough sent me to Carnegie College, near Leeds, to the FA's football school. It was there I first met the future England manager Walter Winterbottom who, even then early in his academic career, had the reputation of being a first class lecturer.

My instructor on the course was Sheffield United's magical North-east born inside-forward Jimmy Hagan, who played many games for England during the war, before becoming a fine manager both in this country and abroad.

It was his enthusiastic style of coaching that probably sparked my interest in teaching the technical aspects of the game later in my career. I took a great interest in the football school and listened to every bit of advice.

On my return to Teesside I purchased my first car, a grand little Morris 8, AUM 981. It's funny how you can always remember your first number plate, it has always stuck in my memory. I've had many vehicles since then, but I can honestly say I had more pleasure from that car, not to mention the romantic moments in the back seat, than all of the others put together.

Although it gave me the freedom to hit the road on a Saturday night to the local North-east dance halls, my social life led to disagreements with my father, especially after I'd been involved in three motoring accidents. Dad wasn't too happy about the late nights I was keeping, and many a time he threatened to put a match inside the Morris's petrol tank.

The crux of the problem was he wanted me to realise that in order to be a successful professional footballer I had to make certain sacrifices and not compromise on my fitness. While I fully understood his concern, I must confess I did over-indulge in all the social benefits of my new status, particularly when I was invited to the liveliest night spots in town.

In the late 1930s Middlesbrough were an excellent and well respected side. They played a brand of passing football which was much admired throughout the country. The team was a well balanced mixture of emerging Mannion and Hardwick youth and reliable Baxter, Cumming, Fenton, Forrest and Milne experience. That combination helped us to finish fifth in the First Division in 1937-38 and fourth a year later. We gave everybody a hard game, and I'm sure that none of our opponents looked forward to playing against us. And we seemed to be getting stronger and more confident every season. Everybody on Teesside believed, as did the players, that the Championship would soon be brought to Ayresome Park for the first time. But the invasive actions of a certain Mr Adolf Hitler put paid to that possibility.

The outbreak of the Second World War caused the suspension of the national football league and the majority of the Boro squad joined the call to arms.

• THREE •

King's Cross? No chance mate

When the Second World War was declared, it was immediately clear that football and other sporting pursuits would have to take a back seat. We were at war with a well-armed and well organised enemy, and the future of our whole country was at stake.

The young men of the country were expected to fight to preserve that future, and it was immediately clear that conscription would be introduced for everybody, regardless of their peacetime occupations. Germany were so much more better equipped than us, that there was a grave danger that we could be invaded at any time. It was a case of all hands to the pump.

However, rather than wait to be formally conscripted, I decided to volunteer for the Royal Air Force at the Middlesbrough recruiting office. I was 19. I had no idea what I was letting myself in for, but neither did any of the thousands of young men who signed up at the same time for the various branches of the Forces. We all felt that we had to do our duty and were ready to hit back at Mr Hitler. It was a time of great anticipation, and strong resolve.

When the official call-up papers arrived I was instructed to report to the Cardington training camp and given the number 943971. I drove myself to Bedfordshire and as I approached the main entrance in my Morris 8, I was greeted at the barrier by two concrete faced, unsmiling sentries.

When I informed them that I was a new recruit, the sarcastic question: "Who do you think you are, the ruddy commanding officer?" was posed. This was followed immediately by the blunt instruction to: "Get out of that car."

I suppose it did appear to be somewhat pretentious arriving in my own car, but I must say that trusty jalopy proved to be an essential mode of both social and professional transportation. Many was the night I squeezed half a dozen friends inside for an evening out, or drove to a variety of venues around the country to play football.

During the first six weeks of training at Cardington, a nine inch layer of snow covered the ground and we were confined to the camp in positively Arctic conditions.

After initial training I went on to the RAF's No 1 Air Gunnery in Manby, Lincolnshire, where, on the firing range, I came out top of my group.

I found I had a good eye for a target, which was probably due to the experience I'd gained during my childhood, shooting duck with my father and Grandad Hardwick.

In fact the squadron leader was so impressed with my results that he confided in me that I was instructor material. I was quite taken aback by his comments, especially as I was only 19 years old. On reflection, however, the squadron leader doubted whether I possessed the necessary physical presence or menace to undertake the job because, in his opinion, I was too baby-faced. I suppose it was not surprising considering I was still a teenager.

However the squadron leader was determined that this would not hold me back. So, in order to make myself look older and more authoritarian, he advised me to grow a moustache. I decided to follow his advice. And from that day to this, I've never shaved my top lip.

After also completing a wireless operators course at RAF Yatesbury in Wiltshire and undergoing parachute training at Ringway, Manchester, I was eventually posted to RAF Binbrook in Lincolnshire as a corporal with 142 and 12th squadrons.

While in Lincolnshire I played couple of games for Grimsby Town and opened the batting for the RAF against the Cranwell Officer Flying School, making a few runs in the process. Life in the services was certainly bearable if you displayed any sort of sporting ability.

From Binbrook we were sent to Eastchurch, on the Isle of Sheppey in Kent. It was a camp best described as an inhospitable marsh, miles from anywhere, and surrounded by sheep grazing land.

Our brief was to observe and report on the build-up of large barges that the Germans were stockpiling on the French coast in anticipation of a possible invasion. However, due to the intense bombing campaign undertaken by the enemy, which put the airfield out of commission for long periods, our Fairy Battle rarely took to the skies.

At the time of my new posting in south-east England I didn't realise how quickly my life would change in so many ways.

My first surprise was when Billy McCracken, the manager of Aldershot, asked me to play for the Southern League team alongside Frank Swift, Cliff Britton, Joe Mercer, Tommy Lawton and Ralph Birkett. Not a bad line-up. The club certainly benefitted from being in close proximity to the services' physical training camp with both the instructors and trainees able to periodically guest for the Shots.

Unfortunately, even though I was playing in such exalted company, the journey back from Hampshire to Eastchurch was a nightmare and I reluctantly had to decline any further invitations to play.

Social life on our isolated airbase mainly revolved around mess room activities and our once a week camp dances. As the base was quite isolated we organised a bus service to provide transport for the local lasses and girls serving in the Auxiliary Territorial Services. And if any extra seating capacity was required, my car was always available with a willing driver.

It was at one of those functions, when I was all "spivved up" in my freshly pressed blue uniform, that I noticed an attractive ATS girl called Joy Bayley and asked her for a dance.

That dance turned out to be longer than I'd anticipated because the pretty gun-setter later became my wife. It was a wartime romance.

Joy was originally from London and the following year we were married in Shoeburyness near Southend with an RAF pal of mine, Stan Ballard, acting as best man. After the wedding we lived in Sheerness, where our first child, Michael, was born in 1943.

My new base was directly on the flight path to London, and very early one morning we awoke to find the sky black with German aircaft. Unfortunately one of their primary targets appeared to be RAF Eastchurch. Within seconds of our rude awakening I was in a shelter, with half a dozen other lads, clad in my pyjamas, with a steel helmet as my only means of protection.

For fifteen minutes they literally blasted hell out of the base. None of our planes had time to even get off the ground to mount a counter attack. The base's only means of defence, three Lewis guns, were about as effective in combat as using a peashooter to stop an elephant.

After the horrendous noise and mayhem had subsided, came the dreadful business of tending to the dead and wounded of which, tragically, there were many. I was experiencing my first real taste of warfare, and it was most unpleasant. Any romanticism about the glory of war quickly disappeared when I viewed the gruesome sights in front of my eyes. I learned very quickly that war was a cruel and evil sickness, and I hope that this country never again has to suffer from the carnage and destruction which is meted out when people fight people.

Meanwhile, by lunchtime, when the initial damage reports had been filed, it was clear that operations from our base were over for a while. The Germans had accomplished their mission. The airfield was pock-marked with craters. Most of our planes had been destroyed. The camp's electricity and water systems were put out of action, and many unexploded bombs littered the site. After the damage assessment was complete, the order came for all senior Non-Commissioned Officers to gather groups of men together, irrespective of their job or trade. We were then instructed to locate all the remaining suspect devices, so they could be safely detonated by the bomb disposal teams.

Until that order was given, I had not fully appreciated what the expression "To have your heart in your mouth" really meant, but mine remained firmly lodged in that position, until the extremely cautious task of locating all the UXBs had been concluded.

Our hard work turned out to be a thorough waste of time, however, because the next morning the base took a similar pounding and the lunar landscape of the previous day was recreated. In all, the incessant blitz on our camp lasted for around eight weeks.

At this juncture, in my recollections, it would be most ungrateful not to mention the voluntary assistance we received from the residents of Sheerness. At the height of the bombing campaign, when the airbase's water and electricity supplies were damaged beyond repair, they unselfishly provided us with food, drink and washing facilities. Their kindness was much appreciated at the time and is still remembered today.

As a result of experiencing my first air raid at Eastchurch I found myself becoming anxious and claustrophobic when entering the temporary shelters. In construction they were nothing more than deep holes excavated out of the ground, covered with corrugated tin sheeting. I felt so helpless and vulnerable just sitting there during a bombing run. Eventually I decided to stay in the open air, curled up in a ditch, and if possible outside the main target area.

On one occasion, as the base was taking yet another aerial pounding, I nervously peered out of my bolthole and noticed that a colleague had been blown off his feet and was lying face down about fifty yards away. When the bombing had ceased, I decided to give him some assistance. As I knelt down by his side he was quite motionless.

Slowly I turned him over and discovered he'd suffered massive internal injuries and was dead. That grim incident again brought home to me how, in times of senseless conflict, the gift of life can become so cheap and worthless.

As the sirens blared out their ear-piercing warning to herald another unwelcome visit from the Luftwaffe, there was no time to reach my usual open air bolthole. So, along with a couple of colleagues I managed to scramble for cover inside the nearest corrugated shelter.

Within seconds of our arrival there was a blinding white flash and a tremendous explosion as the shelter took the brunt of a direct hit. I was thrown sideways amid a maelstrom of flying sandbags and metallic debris.

As the dust settled, and the visibility cleared, I found myself lying flat on my back.

When I finally regained some semblance of my senses, I realised that I'd been hit in both legs by flying shrapnel. Another laddie, who had taken the full force of the blast, was lying motionless across my chest and it wasn't long before I became saturated in the warm blood from his wounds.

The effect of his bodyweight bearing down on me meant I couldn't move, and with my left leg also bent double underneath me, a great strain was placed on my knee joint. I later learned it had sustained serious ligament damage.

Being cocooned below ground in total darkness was a petrifying experience, not knowing whether I would be located before the small pocket of air in which I was breathing ran out.

Suddenly, I then heard a strained voice close by, calling out for help. And after replying to the plea for assistance, I established that my colleague was in a similar position to me, except for one important difference, he was lying next to an unexploded bomb.

Now it was at that time I started praying for the rescue squad to arrive, and quickly.

Although being buried alive was a hugely terrifying ordeal, at that young age you seem to have a zest for survival which, in times of personal crisis, keeps your spirits up and helps you to endure the hardship.

It was on that inner strength I was able to draw, until my dead companion and I were eventually recovered from the mangled shelter some considerable time later.

It is far too obvious to say that my brush with death was a chastening experience I will never forget. Even today, over half a century later, I still find it unnerving to be in confined spaces, such as lifts. But I'm eternally grateful to still be here to recall those traumatic events.

After my rescue I was dispatched for treatment to a stately home in the Kent countryside, which doubled as a military hospital.

Coincidentally, occupying the next bed was a young pilot who I'd extricated from his damaged Spitfire after he'd made a forced landing on what remained of our airfield.

During our long conversations I discovered we were practically next door neighbours, as he lived in Stockton-on-Tees.

Within a couple of weeks the pair of us were equipped with wheelchairs and had many a laugh at each other's inept attempts to control our makeshift mode of transport.

It was while I was receiving treatment at the rather grand Preston Hall, near Maidstone, that I came to fully appreciate, and indeed admire, the wonderful dedicated work done by our nurses. It was a profession I'd previously taken for granted, and I wish to place on record that the care and support I received during my hospitalization was first class.

Even though the hall was quite isolated, it was not immune to German bombing raids. Many times we were wheeled out of our wards by the nurses and pushed into the local woods for our own safety.

Apart from the obvious mental shock and trauma of being buried alive for such a long time, the main physical injury I sustained was to my left knee, which took a terrible beating. The superficial shrapnel wounds I am pleased to say soon healed and posed no long-term problems.

The constant pressure for beds at the hospital meant that once I could move around proficiently with the aid of crutches, I was driven back to Eastchurch in an ambulance to begin my rehabilitation at the base's medical centre.

When I arrived at the camp, wearing the same ragged blood stained uniform I'd been rescued in, I found the place was deserted and the personnel dispersed around the countryside. I eventually located our headquarters in a nearby village.

They took one look at my physical condition, gave me some back pay, and deposited me on the nearest railway station to find my own way home to convalesce.

That decision set in motion another harrowing and lonely sequence of events over which I had no control whatsoever.

My journey home began when I was taken to Sheerness station for the London train, from where I intended to catch the East Coast sleeper at King's Cross for Darlington.

As the train from Kent began to approach the capital it slowed appreciably and, as I looked out of the carriage window, the skyline was illuminated by a strikingly picturesque deep orange glow. The air, in complete contrast, was filled with the stench of black acrid smoke which penetrated everywhere, and made breathing difficult. I had arrived on the outskirts of London during one of the worst nights of the blitz.

We came to an abrupt halt at New Cross station, south of the River Thames. Everybody quickly alighted in order to run for cover, leaving me to struggle with my crutches.

As I surveyed the scene in the distance there were flames dancing everywhere. The city was literally burning down around me. The noise was deafening and it felt like the end of the world had arrived with a vengeance.

The only solution to my immediate predicament was to warily take cover in the pedestrian tunnel below the station.

I spent one hell of a rough night cowering alone in that subway. The bombing never stopped. The fires increased in their intensity, but I was grateful for that temporary shelter, because I had nowhere else to go.

At the time I thought our country would never survive the systematic destruction to which it was being subjected. It seemed that the enemy had so many aeroplanes, and so much hardware, with which to bombard us into submission.

Finally, when the mayhem subsided, I tentatively made my way out of the tunnel, but I didn't have a clue where to go or what to do. Everywhere I looked there was smouldering rubble and burst mains spewing spectacular fountains of water into the air.

I was wandering around rather aimlessly through the decimated streets, when purely by chance an Air Raid Patrol rescue squad, in a flat backed truck, stopped beside me and one of the wardens shouted above the din: "What the hell are you doing out on a night like this?"

I replied that I was trying to get to King's Cross in order to return to the North-east. He was rather perplexed. He told me that I had no chance of reaching the station because the bombing raid had put paid to the immediate possibility of any public transport running.

His reply made me feel depressingly forlorn. However, my melancholic facial expression must have betrayed my innermost thoughts because, to my complete surprise, I was lifted on to the rear of the truck and taken across the city to King's Cross station.

It was a nightmare of a journey which again brought home to me the futility of war. People's homes and businesses were destroyed beyond repair. Lives now permanently ruined. Utter devastation and chaos everywhere I looked.

Once I'd arrived at King's Cross, I was eventually able to complete the final part of my journey to Darlington. It was all thanks to the admirable assistance of the ARP wardens, to whom I conveyed my heartfelt gratitude.

It's nearly sixty years since I was buried alive on that momentous day at Eastchurch and blindly travelled across our blitzed capital city, but I can still vividly recall both those events as if they were yesterday. When you come so close to death, especially at an early age, it's something which becomes rooted in your thoughts for ever.

During those desperate weeks, as Britain battled courageously for its very survival, the dark sinister hand of war touched George Hardwick. They were horrific times for me and for everybody else who was unfortunate to have to suffer and witness those ghastly events. The scenes which I experienced at firsthand will never be erased from my memory.

Once back on Teesside, and my parents had recovered from the shock of a tramp knocking at their door, I reported to Thornaby Aerodrome medical centre, near Stockton-on-Tees, for rehabilitation treatment on my knee. Unfortunately, the type of equipment I needed to aid my recovery was not available. In fact there was nothing in the area which could help me. So, after a detailed consultation to establish my precise requirements, I was transferred to Loughborough College, Leicestershire, where it was hoped that the physical education specialists based there would be able devise a programme to facilitate my recuperation.

When I arrived at Loughborough there was no compassionate diagnosis. No beating about the bush. I was told, very plainly, that such was the severity of the ligament damage to my knee, that in all probability it was unlikely I would play football again.

I was totally devastated. At twenty years of age I just couldn't contemplate a life without football. It was all that I had ever wanted to do. But here I was, being informed in no uncertain terms that this was probably the end of my career. It was over before it had started. It was a crushing statement to hear, and for some time I was in a deep state of shock.

However, after receiving the news of that depressing diagnosis, I worked hard to come to terms with the situation. In fact I became more determined than ever to regain full fitness, and continue with the profession which, apart from my family, meant more to me than anything else in the world.

I needed no motivation, other than to say to myself: "I bloody well will play football again!"

Two of the squadron leaders at Loughborough were the world famous British tennis players, Dan Maskell, and three times Wimbledon singles champion, Fred Perry.

As successful sportsmen themselves, they understood and empathised perfectly with my fervent desire to play again. I am pleased to say I couldn't have received any more positive encouragement than they gave me. I was never given a moment's peace.

The treatment was slow, repetitive, laborious and at times teeth clenchingly painful. I pulled weights and exercised continually to restore the strength to my injured knee.

I did, however, have one great advantage on my side, the keenness of youth, which no doubt contributed to the healing process.

Eventually after many hours of hard graft and assistance from Perry and Maskell, I was discharged. The knee wasn't perfect but the treatment had gone as far as it could in those days. I owed to great debt to the persistence of Perry and Maskell, whose major contribution to my recovery I wish to formally acknowledge,

If the truth be known I always played through the pain barrier from then on. At the start of every match the knee was stiff, and would take a few minutes to loosen up. Once it did, I managed to play an effective part in most matches, by developing a shrewd ability to read the game, and avoid being caught out of position.

After the game, however, the joint would swell appreciably and occasionally had to be supported with a heavy strapping. But the post match discomfort was a small price to pay in order to play again, and I never once thought about the possible long-term health consequences. You don't as a footballer. You just live for the day.

After my treatment at Loughborough was complete, I took a PT instructors' course in the Midlands, which prepared me for what I believe to be my most significant personal contribution to the war effort.

I was placed in charge of an RAF unit based near Maidstone, in Kent. The facility endeavoured to provide constructive rehabilitation treatment for those pilots and gunners whose nerves had been totally shattered by the cumulative effect of flying constant sorties over enemy territory. The levels of the stress they experienced every time they taxied to the end of the runway must have been excruciating. They took to the skies in the knowledge that, not only were they risking their lives, but the odds on their safe return, were very high indeed. They were always in danger of being shot out of the skies, and deprived of the opportunity to return home to their loved ones. Those pilots and gunners displayed tremendous bravery and courage, and their massive contribution to the war effort should never be forgotten.

A relevant point which is often neglected, in my opinion, concerns the psychological impact that their brave actions had on those men.

Although they were at war, and on strategic missions to destroy specific enemy targets, the bombs which they unloaded often killed many innocent civilians. That fatal consequence was a distressing outcome, which many of the pilots found difficult to accept. They could do their very best to aim their bombs at strategic military and industrial targets, but there was always the chance that many innocent people would also die as a result of their sorties.

Due to a lack of pastoral care in the early stages of the war, many of the airmen who buckled under the unceasing pressure were seen as weak individuals. They were often treated with disdain, and their genuine medical condition was unfairly labelled as Lacking in Moral Fibre (LMF). At the time that stigma was tantamount to accusing somebody of cowardice.

Later, however, there was a greater awareness and understanding of their plight, and to meet the needs of those suffering servicemen I was asked to devise a structured rehabilitation scheme.

I was fortunate to start my appointment from a position of strength, because most of the patients knew I was a professional footballer, so I immediately gained their respect.

The project's main objective was to restore individual self-esteem through a positive programme of organised physical activity both in the gym and on the athletics field.

As there were few unbombed areas on the base, I took the lads to the Maidstone running track every day to practise their skills. Soon I had them sprinting, long jumping, pole vaulting and hurdling, with a good deal of success.

The culmination of the course was a grand athletics meeting to which we invited some of the biggest names in the sport, such as the fantastic little miler of that time, Sydney Wooderson.

I believe in some cases I made a small contribution towards the rehabilitation process. But in general, I must acknowledge that it was impossible to eradicate the deep mental scarring that some of the pilots had endured, resulting from their traumatic experiences. I'm sure, like most of us to varying degrees, they carried those deep scars of war for the rest of their lives. It was another harrowing example of the futility and worthlessness of war.

• FOUR •

Somebody called Rous

The outbreak of the Second World War led to an immediate suspension of the national football fixture list. This was not a time to think about sport. The whole future of the country was at stake, and sport had to take a back seat.

However professional sportsmen and women still had a great deal to offer the war campaign and the football authorities put the game's facilities at the disposal of the War Office. The club coaches, trainers, masseurs and hundreds of players became an important human resource for the war effort, tailor-made to improving the physical conditioning of the new conscripts.

Many professionals rapidly established themselves as physical fitness instructors, gaining their qualifications through centres like those at Aldershot, before providing the backbone of the Army Physical Training Corps, and the RAF Physical Training School.

At first, everybody's mind was concentrated on doing everything they could to defy the Germans. Gradually, however, it was realised that sport could still play a part, to a lesser degree, by helping to maintain the morale of the people. So, after the terribly severe winter of 1940, when most grounds were unplayable, football was eventually reorganised into ten regional leagues with a travel restriction of fifty miles imposed on the participating clubs. It was not intended to be competitive football on the scale of what we had been used to enjoying in the 1930s. But it was still important to the people who could come along to watch, especially as many of the country's top players could still be seen displaying their skills. Initially crowds were limited to 25% of a ground's normal capacity, because of air raid regulations, and the games were subject to strict police and local authority control.

By the end of the war, however, the fans were flocking to watch the high profile games. Huge crowds were attracted to matches particularly between England and Scotland at Hampden Park, Glasgow, and London's Wembley Stadium, the latter of which miraculously escaped unscathed during the blitz.

In 1941 I received an invitation to play for Chelsea, who were managed by the former Boro star of the 1920s, Billy Birrell. I was lucky that my superior, Wing Commander Bill Eaves, was a keen football fan, and many a time he allowed me to switch my duty roster in order to play at Stamford Bridge.

From 1941-1945 I made over 75 appearances for The Pensioners, scoring two goals in the process.

I was also fortunate to play in two Southern League wartime cup finals at Wembley, in front of 80,000 spectators. We lost in the final to Charlton Athletic in 1944, but won the following year when our opponents were Millwall.

One Southern League game I can clearly recall took place against Fulham at Craven Cottage.

We were about 15 minutes into the match, when the monotonous drone of the flying bombs called doodle bugs could be heard in the distance, and coming ever closer. The match immediately stopped and everybody in the crowd of 30,000 dived for cover. The players and the officials, however, were left stranded on the pitch, and could only lie down in the mud, until the threat had passed over.

The deadly devices eventually landed some way off on the other side of the Thames, but we still felt the full force of the mammoth explosions. In fact the impacts were so strong, and the ground shook so much, that I thought the stands at Craven Cottage were going to collapse.

A short time after the commotion had died away everybody just stood up, and we continued with the game as if nothing had happened. It was quite an amazing response to what could have been a life threatening situation. The reaction typified the defiant, carry on regardless, spirit which had become prevalent in the country at the time, despite the constant provocation.

Another Chelsea recollection concerns the manager, Billy Birrell, who was summoned one rainy Friday afternoon to Stamford Bridge, and told that the terracing had been struck by an unexploded device.

The general consensus of opinion from the police officers in charge was not promising. Apparently the bomb disposal teams were so hard pressed it was unlikely they would be able to deal with the shell for the best part of a week. That assessment of the situation meant that Chelsea's home game the following day would have to be cancelled.

On hearing their verdict, Birrell's hand suddenly disappeared into the water filled hole. He had no idea what he might find, or if it was potentially explosive. Everybody watched apprehensively as he blindly fiddled about. Then, to the sound of scraping metal, he removed his arm, and triumphantly held aloft the offending shell cap. It was a remarkable act of bravery, considering that he could have been blown to pieces.

The match took place as planned the next day, thanks to the determined efforts of the manager. But the tale also demonstrates the lengths that some people went to in order to ensure football continued uninterrupted.

As the hostilities dragged on, football played an increasingly important role in the war effort, by providing much needed extra finance. Organisations such as the Red Cross and St John's benefitted greatly from the gate receipts generated by international matches. The Football Association also supported many of the benevolent funds established to provide monetary assistance for those who were bereaved or left homeless.

Initially the quality of league football rapidly deteriorated as the professional clubs lost their better players to National Service. Teams often took to the field with a rag bag assortment of local youths and part-timers, to fulfil their outstanding fixtures.

The standard of play, however, gradually improved as many of the home nations' finest footballers, who were stationed around the country, guested for the teams closest to their bases. For example, Sir Matt Busby and Bill Nicholson, the legendary managers of Manchester United and Tottenham Hotspur, played for Middlesbrough.

Without adopting the guest system in the early part of the war, football would have probably collapsed altogether. Its initial implementation had been sanctioned by the authorities to help those clubs survive who were short of players.

Later, the system was deliberately abused by the larger clubs, who saw the acquisition of certain international players as good box-office. Their teamsheets became liberally sprinkled with the names of AN Other, A Newman and SO Else in a vain attempt to hide an individual's true identity.

Some players even played twice in a day to supplement their incomes. Len Shackleton, Sunderland's fine but outspoken England international, made no secret of the fact that one Christmas he turned out for Bradford against Leeds in the morning, had a cup of tea in the dressing-room, and then made his way to play for Bradford City in the afternoon.

The government, to their credit, quickly realised that football could have a positive therapeutic effect on the morale of the nation, especially in the bomb ravaged urban areas, where previous attempts to raise people's spirits, had been confined to a humourless poster campaign urging the population to be more cheerful.

As part of the football initiative, the Board of Trade importantly provided coupons to ensure the continued supply of equipment and production of footballs, which had been hit by the lack of rubber imports from Malaya.

The unprecedented step of even sanctioning Sunday football was also taken at the highest level. The Prime Minister himself, Winston Churchill, was strongly in favour of using sport as a release valve to relieve the tension of war. He gave his official seal of approval to the continuance of football, by attending the international match at Wembley between England and Scotland, in October 1941, and meeting the players prior to the kick off. It was to be his only formal sporting engagement of the war.

Home international and inter-service matches thrived during the war and I represented England and the RAF on many occasions. The games were staged at a variety of venues to ensure that people all over the country had an opportunity to watch some top class football. The players themselves eventually became valuable morale-boosting assets, and although we received only a standard match fee of thirty shillings (£1:50), it was still a privilege to be chosen for your country's international matches.

Despite the backdrop of the war, standards of behaviour, both on and off the pitch, had to be maintained. Discipline was very strict and directives issued by FA secretary, Stanley Rous, who did more than any other official to ensure the continuance of the game during that period by liaising with the Home Office, were discharged by the wartime captains Stan Cullis, Joe Mercer and Eddie Hapgood. Anybody who didn't tow the line was formally reprimanded.

I remember Tommy Lawton, the great Everton and Chelsea centre-forward, speaking out in public about the paltry match fee we were receiving, and then finding himself dropped for having the temerity to pass a personal opinion.

For my part, I appreciated I was very lucky to be at home playing football, because there were thousands of men and woman fighting for their lives, and ours, overseas. That stark reality enabled me to put everything else into perspective. I knew that I was making my own personal contribution to the war effort. But the big advantage was that I was still at home and working near my family. That was a benefit which many members of the British armed forces did not have the opportunity to enjoy, particularly the soldiers in the army who were away from their loved ones for months and even years on end. In this respect, I was definitely one of the lucky ones.

Under those circumstances I would have gladly played football for nothing, and probably did most of the time, because trying to get travelling expenses from the FA was a nightmare. Their treasurer appeared to know, down to the last halfpenny, the cost of fares and your claim forms were often returned with a curt "Too Much" scrawled across them.

I can emphatically assure the reader that the standard of play in the wartime international matches was tremendous. I know, I participated in most of them.

Just because the games have never received formal recognition from the statisticians does not mean they were lacking in quality. Granted, we were not playing for British Championship points, but that meant there was no pressure to get a result. The players, therefore, were more relaxed and displayed their natural instinctive talents and skills to entertain the fans.

Neither was it just exhibition football, as some of the most bruising and physical encounters I ever played in, took place during the war.

I certainly feel the game as a whole benefitted from the more open style of football, because you were always playing with, and against, the best. That benefit transferred itself to international level when, in the late 1940s, England had a terrific side capable of destroying teams 10-0.

Unfortunately for me, and many of the illustrious players of that era, we lost six seasons out of our careers, and in some cases they were the best years of our chosen profession. Those players affected included some of the greatest footballing legends of all time: Eddie Hapgood, Joe Mercer, Stan Cullis, Cliff Britton, Wilf Mannion, Raich Carter, Johnny Carey, Tommy Lawton, Frank Swift, Bill Shankly, Matt Busby and Torry Gillick.

Regrettably, the football record books choose to ignore these very competitive international matches, which were played between 1941 and 1945. They appear to be of no significance or worth. Also, as no caps were awarded for the matches, they are not permitted to count on your official international record. That is a situation which I feel is unfair considering the number of games some of us played, in order to provide entertainment through those bleak years.

Having resumed my playing career with Chelsea I was relaxing in the mess room at Eastchurch when one of the lads appeared at the main door and called out: "George... telephone, somebody called Rous about football."

As I picked up the receiver I was racking my brains to think of who I knew by that name from Stamford Bridge, when the caller identified himself as Stanley Rous, the secretary of the Football Association.

He then proceeded to invite me to take the place of the injured England full back, Eddie Hapgood, in the forthcoming international match at the City Ground, Nottingham, against Wales. The date was April 1941 and I was only 21. I couldn't believe it. At first I thought it was some tasteless prank, and that one of the many comedians around me was playing a huge joke on me. However, after Mr Rous confirmed my selection for the third time, I was finally convinced the call was genuine.

I was overjoyed by the news and literally ran to see Bill Eaves for permission to travel to the game. He was almost as pleased me, and even gave me two extra cans of petrol for the journey to Nottingham to the team hotel. It took a long time for the news to sink in. I never imagined in a million years that I was considered good enough at that stage of my development to represent my country at full international level. However, Mr Rous had every faith in me and so had the selectors. So I quickly became determined to give a good account of myself and hopefully play well enough to stay in the team.

The talented England line-up for my first international was: Vic Woodley, Joe Bacuzzi, George Hardwick, Cliff Britton, Stan Cullis (capt), Joe Mercer, Alf Kirchen, Len Goulden, Don Welsh, Jimmy Hagan, Reggie Smith.

We won the game very comfortably by 4-1 with the aptly named Don Welsh, of Charlton Athletic, scoring all four goals.

An added bonus for me, was that my parents were able to travel to Nottingham and witness my big day. This time they did not have to suffer the embarrassment of seeing me score an own goal. In fact I was quite satisfied after the game with my overall performance and developed a hunger for more.

My immediate opponent at outside-left in the international was Dai Hopkins of Brentford, and you never came off the field unscathed after playing against Dai. He was a very tough customer, who made his presence felt. I ended up with a couple of stitches in my bottom lip and a laceration to my knee. But I didn't mind. I revelled in that first game for England. It was another dream come true following my professional debut for Middlesbrough.

For me to gain international recognition after those long arduous weeks of rehabilitation on my injured knee, not knowing for certain whether I'd even play again in the top flight, was a fitting tribute to the hard work, patience and dedication of Dan Maskell and Fred Perry, to whom I was deeply indebted.

During the war the rivalry with Scotland was just as intense and fierce as it always had been, and the public flocked in their thousands to watch the encounters.

The first time I played against Scotland was at Hampden Park, in April 1943, as a member of this fine England team which lined up: Frank Swift, George Hardwick, Leslie Compton, Cliff Britton, Stan Cullis, Joe Mercer, Stan Matthews, Raich Carter, Dennis Westcott, Jimmy Hagan, Denis Compton.

The unofficial attendance of over 100,000 was, until then, the largest crowd I'd witnessed in my career. In fact, so many fans wanted to see the game that the gates were stormed, leading to some unfortunate injuries in the resultant crush.

Considering it was my first experience of the intimidating Glasgow atmosphere, I thought I acquitted myself quite well, and my own assessment was confirmed when I read the press reports the following day which said:

"The England defence was much improved and full-back Hardwick was a success."

I was very pleased with those comments, taking into account I played out of position at right-back, in order to accommodate Arsenal's Leslie Compton on the other flank.

My travelling companion to Glasgow was my immediate opponent, the Scottish outside-left Billy Liddell of Liverpool, so loved and respected on Merseyside. He too was in the RAF and stationed in the South of England.

My main memories of the game were, firstly, that it was the only time I ever saw Raich Carter shed his normally nonchalant attitude and crack his poker face for a brief moment on the field of play.

Early in the game, like most teams buoyed up by the home support, Scotland were piling on the pressure, and gained a corner on the right. As it was crossed into our box, one of the Scots lads flashed in a glorious header which was flying towards the top corner of our net.

As usual I'd taken up my customary position on the goal line and somehow managed to find enough spring in my legs to deflect the ball over the crossbar.

To my amazement Raich ran from the edge of the penalty area, threw his arms around me, planted a kiss firmly on my cheek, and said: "Well done son."

Never again did I see him show any outward signs of emotion. Even when he frequently scored with his 25 yard specials from outside the box. In fact, he hit the first two goals in our 4-0 victory that day and didn't make the slightest fuss.

The second incident of note occurred near full-time and involved our captain, Stan Cullis, who was standing in a defensive wall ready to face a Scottish free kick.

As he was organising our line, he suddenly collapsed on the turf, writhing in agony, with his shorts torn. The Wolves centre-half had something of a reputation for being a hard man, so it was quite a surprise to see him taken from the field in obvious pain, clutching his groin.

Only when we returned to the dressing-room did we discover the full extent of what had actually happened.

Apparently one of the Scottish forwards, Dougie Wallace, had taken a shine to Cullis's genitals and squeezed them so tight that he'd fallen to the ground with the ferocity of the unwelcome attention. It was no laughing matter.

The eye watering injury turned out to be quite serious, with Cullis having to wear a surgical support when he played. Later, after a formal investigation, the culprit, Wallace, was never selected again for Scotland.

Some football commentators have stated that the systematic 8-0 demolition of Scotland, at Maine Road, Manchester, in October 1943, was one of England's finest ever performances. I tend to disagree.

When making a claim like that you need to take into account the standard of the opposition, and on the day we were playing a rather weak Scottish side.

The match, however, was still a triumph for the unassuming Stanley Matthews. In fact I had so little to do in the defensive half of the field that I had time to admire the mercurial skills and body swerve of The Wizard of the Dribble. Time and time again we just passed the ball to Stan and off he went down the wing, to torment the hard-pressed Scottish full-back Miller, before setting up a host of chances for our forwards.

Finally, after helping Tommy Lawton to score four times, Stan delivered his own *coupe de grace* by beating man after man before rounding the punch-drunk goalkeeper, Crozier, for a stunning individual goal.

Stan continued his mercurial form in February 1944 against Scotland at Wembley, where prior to the kick-off, I had the honour of being presented by our captain, Stan Cullis, to King George VI.

The match was also attended by many other distinguished dignitaries, including The Queen, Princess Elizabeth, King Haakon of Norway, Deputy Prime Minister Clement Attlee and General Montgomery. It was indeed a regal occasion.

After two previous heavy defeats against England, by 4-0 and 8-0, the Scottish selectors introduced many younger players to their team in an attempt to halt our total dominance of the fixture.

A debutant, Jimmy Stephen, who played for Bradford, was given the unenviable task of marking Matthews, not the type of player you'd chose to oppose when making your first international appearance.

During the first half Stephen acquitted himself admirably, leaving Stan little room in which to manoeuvre, and by the interval the game was nicely poised at 1-1.

Early in the second period saw the mistake which turned the match, when Scottish full-back Macauley deflected a shot past his own goalkeeper, Crozier. The error seemed to deflate the Scots' resistance and with Matthews in full flow, Tommy Lawton, Jimmy Hagan, Joe Mercer and Raich Carter quickly scored the goals to put the game beyond Scotland's reach.

We eventually ran out comfortable winners 6-2 with Matt Busby disconsolately accepting, in his post match comments as Scottish captain, that we were again the better side but hadn't deserved to win by such a large margin.

Another match against Scotland, which coincidentally finished in the same score-line, 6-2, took place in October 1944 and was of great personal significance.

I vividly remember the game because Bob Baxter, Dave Cumming and myself were all selected to play in the same Wembley international.

Although opposing my mentor, Bob Baxter, was a real thrill, I certainly had no intention of passing him the ball, bloody quick. I'd grown up a bit since those days. For Middlesbrough, it was also an achievement to have three of their players in the same representative match. It was a statistic which I'm sure created a club record.

The game itself was much closer than the final result suggests because for about an hour the Scots played really well and held a deserved 1-0 lead. Then they were hit by a second half whirlwind in the masterful shape of Tommy Lawton, who turned the match in our favour with a timely hat-trick and supplied further goals for Raich Carter, Len Goulden and Jimmy Hagan.

The match also saw the international debut of Darlington's young centre-half Bob Thyne, who was surprisingly called up instead of Matt Busby, when the future manager of Liverpool, Bill Shankly, failed a fitness test. Thyne, who was recovering from shrapnel wounds and had to borrow Shanks's kit in order to play, received a harsh baptism into international football.

In the autumn of 1944 I made my first trip abroad, to Belgium, with the Combined Services. The team, captained by Matt Busby, included Frank Swift, Eddie Hapgood, Bernard Joy, Joe Mercer, Stan Matthews, Raich Carter Tommy Lawton, Maurice Edelstone and Reggie Smith.

We enjoyed convincing victories in Liege and Bruges and by the time we arrived in Brussels our reputations had gathered so much momentum that the demand to see the game was reminiscent of the English FA Cup Final. Everywhere we went in the city the British Army and RAF personnel constantly asked us for tickets. But with the proceeds of the match being donated to the Belgian Refugee Fund they were at a premium, and unfortunately we couldn't help.

During our stay the Belgian FA were very hospitable indeed, providing congenial after match dinners, and escorting us on a tour of every risqué night club in town.

I remember one local Burgomaster producing two crates of champagne, which he'd hidden underneath his cellar floor from the occupying German troops, and generously sharing its particularly potent contents with us for a very agreeable celebratory drink. There were some "happy" footballers on board our transport that night, I can tell you.

We were also taken to a local whippet racing track and given the hot tips for the night. Surprisingly they all won, so the lads received some unexpected extra francs with which to buy presents.

In addition to our winnings, Matt Busby, as skipper, was presented with a young whippet which was to be used as the team mascot. We were instantly taken by the dog, which was our constant companion wherever we went for the remainder of the trip, wining and dining with us at all the best restaurants.

We did give it a name, but I can't for the life of me remember what it was. Unfortunately due to quarantine restrictions we had to leave our canine friend with the RAF lads based at Brussels airport, before we boarded our Dakota to fly home.

The match in Brussels was watched by thousands of British troops who cheered us on to an easy victory. It was also significant for an amazing coincidence which was beyond belief.

Our goalkeeper, Frank Swift, had received a letter from a lady in Chorley, Lancashire, asking him to look out for her son, Charlie Smith, and to tell him it was about time he put pen to paper and wrote home.

She gave Frank no regiment nor rank with which to identify her son, so the chance of locating wayward Charlie from Chorley was virtually nil.

Anyway, towards the end of the match in Brussels, Swifty was walking back towards the crowd about to take a goal kick, when he shouted out as loud as he could: "Is there anybody here called Charlie Smith from Chorley?"

To our utter disbelief, an embarrassed little voice from deep within the crowd piped up: "Yeah, that's me."

Swifty told him to come around to the dressing-room after the match where he presented young Charlie with his mum's letter, and then proceeded to rollick the poor lad for not writing home. Honestly it's a true story.

After a couple weeks back at our bases in England, the Combined Services team were asked to fly to Paris for an exhibition match.

When we arrived at RAF Northholt the two Anson aircraft provided for our flight were so old they could have been autographed by those pioneering aviators from the turn of the century, Orville and Wilbur Wright.

Then, to cap it all, walking towards us we saw an unkempt, dishevelled figure, sporting a large pair of dark glasses to cover the effects of a recently attended all night party. It was our pilot.

I must admit we were all a little sceptical about the sanity of the flight, given the questionable airworthiness of both the plane and its "delicate" captain.

As we squeezed nervously on board, I ended up sitting in the co-pilot's seat, and found myself making a major contribution towards keeping the old crate in the air. I was handed the task of pumping up the under carriage after take-off, by our red-eyed leader. I made sure that I did the job as well as I could, because it was always at the back of my mind that the plane did not have a long life ahead of it. To this day, I don't know how the overloaded Anson became airborne or managed to maintain a height of 750 feet on the journey across the channel.

Our arrival, and unscheduled early departure from Paris airport, was a hair-raising experience, with Hardwick in the forefront of the action.

As we made our not so smooth descent, the pilot suddenly realised we were about to overshoot the runway and yelled at me to pump up the undercarriage as quickly as possible. Now, if there had been a world record for pumping up an undercarriage I wouldn't have broken it. I'd have completely shattered it, without a doubt.

As we hastily aborted our landing, the veteran aircraft began to struggle to maintain its altitude, and we missed a block of flats, about half a mile from the airport, only by banking steeply around them. Having almost lost all our height, the pilot, who by now was miraculously cured of his hangover and needed all of his senses to prevent a disaster, somehow managed to effect a roller coaster of a landing at the second attempt.

The minute the old Anson came to a jolting halt on the runway, several green-faced famous footballers quickly disembarked, and knelt on the ground gratefully kissing good old terra-firma. The little ecclesiastical gathering also included the pilot, who by that time, was bent double being violently ill. It was a flight to remember.

The rapturous welcome we received in France soon restored the normal colour back to our cheeks. In the Parisian streets we were stopped by many restaurant owners declaring that, for us, their food and wine was on the house. It was a very generous gesture with which we were happy to comply.

Prior to the tour, most of the lads were under strict instructions from their wives and girlfriends to bring back items which were rationed in England, such as nylons, underwear and perfume.

I still can picture the giant frame of Frank Swift parading up and down an exclusive lingerie shop modelling an outsize bra, much to the amusement of the manager. Somehow I don't think the Manchester City goalkeeper would have dared act in similar manner in an English high street.

The match was played in a festival atmosphere at the Parc de Princes, against a full strength French national side. We recorded a 5-1 victory and were hailed as The Masters of Football by the home supporters, who were just so relieved that their lives were returning to some sort of normality after liberation.

The stadium itself, however, still displayed the barbed wire remnants of the German occupation, when it was used as a prisoner of war camp.

The return journey home in a more modern Dakota was, thank goodness, uneventful. It was just as well, because I don't think any of us would happily have boarded another Anson. Not with our old pilot on board anyway. We would probably have preferred to swim home.

However our trip was a very successful one. After those two initial excursions abroad, the demand for us to entertain the troops was so overwhelming, that the FA sent out teams overseas on a regular basis until the end of the war.

Back at home I was still playing for Chelsea, and after a good run in the Southern League Cup competition, we'd reached the semi-final stage against Tottenham Hotspur.

The game was played at White Hart Lane, and it was one of those sublime days you occasionally get in football when everything you try comes off. In addition to making our two goals, with surging runs into the Spurs penalty area, every shot or header that beat our keeper, Vic Woodley, I managed to block or clear off the line. My luck was right in, and my performance was given due acclaim in the press as we reached the cup final. After the match one London newspaper had a headline proclaiming:

"Young Hardwick takes Chelsea to Wembley."

The Chelsea fans were wonderful towards the guest players, showing their appreciation for our achievement by sending us gifts of shirts, fruit, petrol and clothing coupons, which I thought was very kind.

On another occasion, outside Stamford Bridge, I was chatting to a supporter about how I was trying to introduce golf to our RAF camp, but was having difficulty finding suitable sets of clubs and balls with which to practice.

By the following home game I'd totally forgotten about the golfing conversation. But, as I arrived at the players' entrance, my memory soon returned. I saw the same chap with his friends weighed down with numerous sets of clubs, bags and balls. In fact they had enough equipment to open my own driving range. Where they'd come from I didn't enquire, but it was still a generous gesture and typical of the Chelsea supporters at that time.

Before our second successive Wembley appearance, we stayed at Sunningdale Golf Course, from where we travelled to the stadium to meet our opponents, Millwall.

We'd been beaten in the final the previous season, 3-1 by Charlton Athletic, when their goalkeeper Sam Bartram had played a blinder, in a game spoilt by persistent heavy rain. At the end of that match I'd climbed the stairs to the royal box and received my loser's mementos from General Dwight D. Eisenhower, Commander-in-Chief of the Allied Forces in Europe.

In our side for the return visit to the twin towers was George

All my kind-hearted grandparents, Alfred and Georgina Moutrey (above) and
Francis and Hannah Hardwick.

Grandad Hardwick, ready for action with
Guisborough C.C. in 1905.

I was always fortunate to be the centre of attention with my mother, Doris and father, Frank.

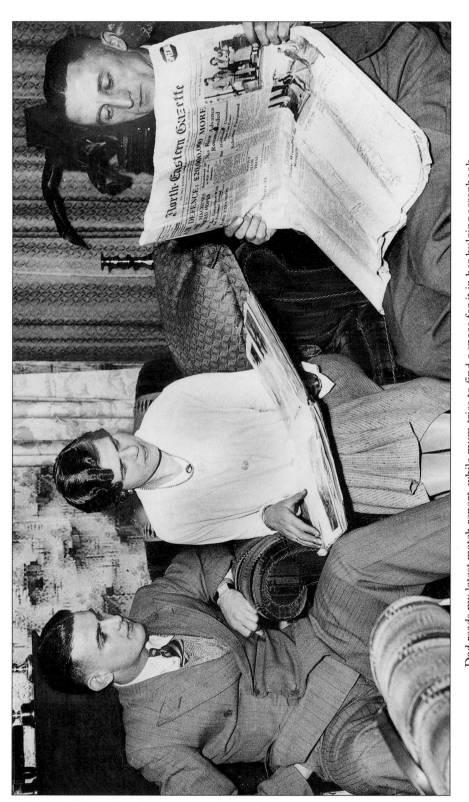

Dad reads my latest match report, while mum tries to find a space for it in her bulging scrapbook.

Happy footballing memories of Lingdale School. As a junior (above), I'm first left in the back row, and as a teenager, I'm seated directly behind the cup.

Youthful snaps in the quartered colours of South Bank East End, (left)
and as a fresh-faced professional at Middlesbrough FC.

My first derby match, Middlesbrough v Sunderland, Ayresome Park, New Year's Day 1938.
I'm pictured third left, between my mentor, Bob Baxter, and a young, Wilf Mannion.

Cutting a dash in my RAF uniform at Cardington (above left).
Standing against my pride and joy, the Morris 8, AUM 981 (above right),
and ready for action after initial training.
(below, middle row, fifth left).

Stan Matthews, (front row, first left), and Stan Mortensen (front row, third left), join me on a wartime RAF team. Mick Fenton, my Boro colleague, is to my left.

The Chelsea team of 1944 containing the future England manager, Ron Greenwood, (back row, centre, in uniform), and managed by the ex-Boro forward, Billy Birrell, in the hat.

A very proud personal moment, as England captain, Stan Cullis, introduces me to King George before the international against Scotland, at Wembley, February 1944.

Overseas stadiums were full to capacity when British representative sides travelled abroad. This team, captained by Matt Busby contains amongst others GH, (fourth left), Stan Mortensen, (first right) and Tommy Lawton, (fifth right).

Talking tactics with England manager Walter Winterbottom are : (left to right),
Frank Swift, GH, Stan Mortensen and Wilf Mannion.

The first England team I captained was against N.Ireland, in Belfast, September 1946.
To my left is Wilf Mannion who scored a hat trick in our 7-2 victory.

The ultimate accolade for every professional footballer,
wearing the international shirt of his country.

In the 1940s George Hardwick was football's equivalent of Clark Gable. (JW)

The FA tour party, summer 1947. Not a bad little squad including Tommy Lawton,
Frank Swift, GH, Dicky Robinson, Wilf Mannion, Billy Wright, Tom Finney, Raich Carter,
Stan Matthews, Neil Franklin, Laurie Scott, Stan Mortensen and Eddie Lowe.

The England team which gave a superlative display of attacking football to beat
Portugal 10-0 in Lisbon, May 1947.

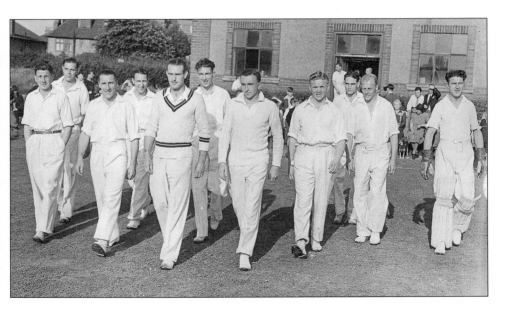

Leading Middlesbrough FC onto the field, with Jimmy Gordon (left), and
Ronnie Dicks (right), for a charity cricket match.

Long-serving Boro trainer Charlie Cole, (left), is kept waiting on the first tee while
Jimmy Gordon, (uniform), and George Dews select their clubs.

Everything appears to be under control as I head clear a Manchester United attack, watched by Boro players' Harry Bell, Wilf Mannion and Dicky Robinson.

Being in the thick of the action was a situation I always relished.

No wonder Bill Whitaker, (left), and Dicky Robinson, (hands on knees), look shattered because we're being thrashed 7-0 by the Arsenal. Our goalkeeper, Bobbie Anderson, made his only Boro appearance in this match at Highbury.

"This way to the platform George." Rolando Ugolini, watched by Johnny Spuhler and Harry Bell, makes sure I catch the train after I'd failed to reach the station for a previous away trip due to unforeseen circumstances.

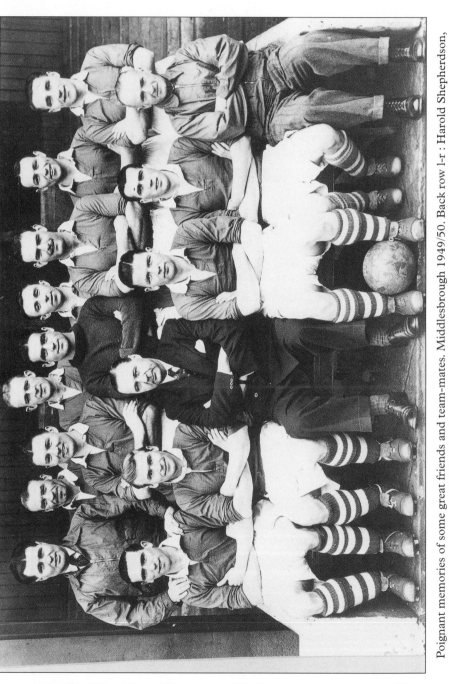

Poignant memories of some great friends and team-mates. Middlesbrough 1949/50. Back row l-r : Harold Shepherdson, Tommy Blenkinsopp, Harry Bell, Bill Whitaker, Rolando Ugolini, Ronnie Dicks, GH, Johnny Spuhler, Jimmy Gordon. Front row : Billy Linacre, Wilf Mannion, David Jack (manager), Peter McKennan, Alex McCrae, Tom Mayson (trainer).

Wardle, who'd signed professional forms for Middlesbrough at the same time as me.

In fact the team which represented the Pensioners that day should have really been called an FA Select XI, such was the diversity of the players' backgrounds. Our side for the final read:

Ian Black (Hearts), Danny Winter (Bolton), George Hardwick (Middlesbrough), Bobbie Russell (Chelsea), Johnny Harris (Wolves), Dickie Foss (Chelsea), George Wardle (Exeter), Len Goulden (West Ham), Joe Payne (Chelsea), Ian McDonald (Bournemouth) and Leslie Smith (Brentford).

On the day we played well, eventually running out comfortable winners by 2-0, with George Wardle scoring one of the goals. The only disappointment, however, was that we didn't receive any medals acknowledging our victory. Plaques and saving certificates were the mementos we received from King George VI, who attended the match with Princess Elizabeth.

A play-off game was then arranged against the northern winners, Bolton Wanderers, to find the national cup champions. We were quite confident, but surprisingly lost 3-2 in front of 65,000 spectators at Stamford Bridge.

I was privileged to play at Wembley on numerous occasions but the turf, despite its pristine and well manicured appearance, was not the easiest of pitches on which to play football. The grass, being very lush, was really hard on the legs and tended to sap the stamina. Your boots also sank deep into the earth and if you weren't careful in your movements, particularly when turning with the ball, you could sustain serious knee and ankle ligament damage.

Down the years, some of the results in the FA Cup Final have been affected by what was described as The Wembley Hoodoo, when in truth it was the constitution of the pitch that probably contributed to the injuries.

Being stationed in southern England, and playing well for Chelsea, certainly enhanced my international prospects. However, the memories of one game against Scotland had nothing to do with any events on the pitch. What the match perfectly illustrated was the strange mix of sentiments that were often associated with playing football during the war.

Picture the scene of 134,000 raucous Scotsmen assembled at Hampden Park, in April 1945, hoping to witness a Scottish victory over the auld enemy for the first time in over three years.

As the teams lined-up, prior to the start of the match, the vast throng all removed their hats in unison, and stood in deferential silence. The sombre tones of the Last Post then resonated around the stadium in tribute to Mr Franklin D. Roosevelt, the President of the USA, who had died the previous day. Nobody moved. There wasn't a sound.....until the muffled drone of a lone Lancaster bomber flew overhead and respectfully dipped its wings, to complete the ceremony. The emotion of the occasion brought a lump to the throat.

Then, once the whistle blew, normal service was resumed and the vociferous, antagonistic, jocular Scottish support filled the air.

The passionate home supporters couldn't, however, help their team record a victory. We were on fire that day as every English forward scored, with Raich Carter and Stan Matthews outstanding in a 6-1 win. And to complete the Scots' misery, Frank Swift even saved a penalty from Matt Busby.

In May 1946, England were invited to play France in Paris to formally celebrate the end of the hostilities.

Following the comprehensive defeat inflicted by the Combined Services side, eighteen months previously, the French players were ready for revenge. They were what I believe in modern sporting circles is termed, "up for it."

The game was very physical indeed with their robust centre-forward Ben Barek persistently throwing his considerable frame in the direction of our debutant goalkeeper Bert Williams, who received no protection at all from a very lenient referee.

In fact the official should have disallowed the opening score, when Barek deliberately flattened Williams seconds before the ball entered the net.

Playing against eleven men is often difficult enough, but when the opposition have an extra man in black on their side as well, your job becomes doubly demanding.

We managed to equalise soon after the restart, when Jimmy Hagan rounded off a great move between himself and Tommy Lawton with a fine strike to beat the French keeper Da Rui, who I would face again when he was chosen to represent the Rest of Europe, at Hampden Park, in April 1947.

The score remained 1-1 until about ten minutes from the end when Bert Williams came to claim a cross only to find himself, and the ball, barged into the net, yet again, by Ben Barek.

The referee saw nothing wrong with deliberate foul challenge and signalled a goal.

At the end of the match poor Bert, who was almost in tears at the injustice of the decision, was all for taking a poke at Barek, and who could blame him. Apart from the criminal decision suffered by Middlesbrough in an FA Cup quarter final against Burnley in 1947, it was one of the most outrageous refereeing decisions I'd ever witnessed.

Three days after that rare England defeat in Paris, Stan Matthews, Neil Franklin and myself flew to Copenhagen. From there we were to board a connecting flight to Oslo, and join up with the rest of an RAF tour party who had already sailed to the Norwegian capital from South Shields on the River Tyne.

About half an hour en route to Scandinavia, I had a strange feeling of *déjà vu* as our ageing aircraft flew into a terrific electrical storm. Not surprisingly the eventful flight to Paris for the Combined Services match flashed through my mind. It was like the Anson flight with the hungover pilot all over again.

This time our plane received a tremendous buffeting from the weather, and we discovered the true meaning of the word turbulence. We proceeded to perform every possible aerial contortion known to stunt fliers, short of the wings falling apart. Everybody on the flight was decidedly queasy, particularly Stan Matthews, who was sitting next to me.

In fact poor Stan was so violently ill, that by the time we reached our destination, his clothes were soaked in perspiration. Thank goodness that on our arrival, we were kindly driven straight to our hotel by members of the Danish FA.

Once at reception, we were given our room keys and informed that, unfortunately, there was a hotel laundry strike in

Copenhagen. Naturally the reception staff told us that they hoped it wouldn't spoil our stay.

To be frank, the domestic information went in one ear and out the other, because all I wanted to do was clean up in preparation for a night out on the town as guests of our Danish hosts.

As I entered the room and put my bag on the nearest of the twin beds, I detected a strange rustling sound coming from beneath the covers. Being an inquisitive sort of a bloke, I pulled back the blankets to discover stiff paper sheets on the bed. It was then that I remembered the receptionist's comments about the laundry problems.

Quick as a flash, I dived over to the other bed to find it contained soft linen sheets. I then placed my pyjamas on the pillow to indicate the bed was mine. It was a case of first come, first served. When a pale and ghostly looking Stan gingerly arrived a few minutes later, he failed to notice anything untoward and accepted the choice of beds without suspicion.

After a great night out, we returned to our hotel just after midnight and Stan soon discovered his musical sheets. Naturally I pretended to be as surprised as he was. However, if I thought my quick thinking in switching beds was going to lead to a comfortable night's sleep, I was very much mistaken. Every time that Stan turned over, his sheets crackled so much that the sound woke us both up. In the end we abandoned the idea of trying to sleep, and talked instead.

Eventually, after exhausting all the topics of conversation, Stan decided to occupy his time by drafting his newspaper column, but couldn't find any writing paper on the dressing table. I then suggested he was crazy to look for paper when he was lying on reams of the stuff. Why look for paper when you can write on your bedsheets?

So, that week Stan Matthews, one of the most famous footballers in the country, avidly read by millions of supporters, wrote his news copy on a crumpled piece of Danish bedsheet.

Next morning, feeling rather weary, we caught the flight to Oslo and joined the rest of the RAF lads, including my Boro team-mate Mick Fenton.

For the duration of the trip we were under the watchful

stewardship of Squadron Leader Jimmy Jewell, the pre-war cup final referee, who went on to become manager of Norwich City. The hospitality we received from the Norwegian people was first class and I particularly remember enjoying the thick tender venison steaks.

After winning all of our three matches in Norway, we moved onto Sweden, which had been completely untouched by the ravages of war. The Stockholm shops were laden with goods we'd never seen for years, particularly clothing. We immediately thought of our wives and girlfriends back home and realised that we could not miss this wonderful shopping opportunity. Poor Jimmy Jewell had to "sub" the lads some extra money so they could buy another suitcase to carry their purchases home.

We managed a win and a draw from our two matches in Sweden and concluded our tour with further victories in Denmark, where I was introduced to the delights of horse trotting. I was so successful that I managed to back three winners.

The tour had been completed undefeated. It had been a marvellous social experience, free from the worries of war, and we had preserved the credibility of English football in the eyes of our Scandinavian hosts.

I have often been asked whether my wartime experiences changed me. The answer is that I certainly grew up quickly in the forces and had learned to take responsibility. But there again, so did many other people. It was character building. Officers were quickly made out of boys. They simply had to be. When orders were issued, you obediently carried them out because you had been trained to do so.

The war "made" many individuals, particularly women, who often had to take on heavy industrial or artillery duties while the men were in action overseas, and they coped admirably.

Although any war is a dreadful period in people's lives, and I saw many of my dear friends in the RAF fly out on sorties from which they never returned, there are some very positive side effects. What develops is a unity of purpose and a spirit of companionship, the latter of which was particularly prevalent among the footballers. We all became extremely close, and even to this day I still receive mail and telephone calls, around Christmas time, from the friends I made over 50 years ago in the services.

Football as an industry, like so many others, paid a terrible price during the war. Thousands of players lost the best years of their careers and hundreds more were either killed in action or so badly injured that they could not rejoin their clubs once the hostilities had ceased.

George Hardwick was one of the lucky ones and I've never forgotten it.

When the Germans eventually surrendered, and I'd recovered from a D-day celebration which lasted two full days, I was offered a commission in the Royal Air Force. It was an honour to be awarded this commission, and under different circumstances I would have been sorely tempted to accept it. I had adapted to life in the forces. So had my family. I declined the invitation, however, because returning to professional football was too big an attraction.

• FIVE •

Captaincy, Controversy and Transfer.

After being demobbed, my return to Teesside with Joy and Mike was not without its minor complications. In an ambitious attempt to acquire my services, Chelsea had offered Middlesbrough the opportunity to name their transfer price and for a time I did not know if we would be staying in the south or returning to the North-east.

However, I had matured into one of the top defenders in the country during the war years, and the Boro directors clearly did not want to lose any of their major assets. So Chelsea's bid was turned down flat and the issue was closed. Although I had enjoyed my time at Stamford Bridge under Billy Birrell, I accepted the Middlesbrough board's decision and resumed my professional career at Ayresome Park.

When I finally reported for training along with Mick Fenton, Harold Shepherdson, Dave Cumming and Bobby Stuart for the 1945/46 season, one of the local lads who had played a few games for the first team before the war was sadly no longer with us. Dave Murphy, who had played with Wilf Mannion at South Bank St Peters, had unfortunately been killed in action.

Northern regional football was well under way and in one of the early away games at Newcastle United I played against a young man called Jackie Milburn who was fresh from the local leagues and had a burgeoning reputation.

Using my experience, I managed to stop him from scoring, as we secured a creditable 1-1 draw at St James' Park. But as the years went by, it became more and more difficult to keep Wor Jackie off the scoresheet. Milburn was the possessor of superb all-round skills and developed into one of the finest centre-forwards this country has ever produced.

In January 1946, the FA Cup competition recommenced in a new two-legged format, and we were drawn away in the third round against Leeds United. Thousands of Boro fans made the journey to Elland Road to watch us draw 4-4 in a real thriller, with newly signed George Dews scoring twice.

During the war, Dews, who was also a county standard cricketer, had been stationed in the army at Whitby and was given a trial at Ayresome Park. By half-time he'd made such an impression that the Boro manager apparently signed him in the interval and he continued to play for Middlesbrough when professional football resumed.

The following week, in the return leg at Ayresome Park, there was no stopping us, as we thrashed our Yorkshire neighbours 7-2, with Mick Fenton completing a hat-trick, and a chap called Hardwick scoring with an extremely well-placed penalty.

In the fourth round we were paired with Blackpool and the tie turned out to be an epic encounter. We lost a closely fought first leg 3-2 away at Bloomfield Road, in which our goalkeeper Dave Cumming played a blinder. Afterwards Mick Fenton couldn't remember anything about the match because of concussion.

The second leg at Ayresome Park kicked off at 2:15pm and by 5pm we were still playing, in almost total darkness, with the aggregate scores locked at 5-5.

In all, we played for 150 minutes, including extra-extra time, before exhaustion and the gathering gloom caused the referee to abandon the match. In those days, there were no floodlights and it became impossible to see the ball in the darkness. To this day it is the longest single match in which Middlesbrough have been involved. The fans certainly got their money's worth that afternoon.

The stalemate meant that in order to decide the tie, a third game had to take place at the neutral venue of Elland Road, Leeds. That match developed into an equally tense encounter.

The Yorkshire ground was packed to the rafters with a crowd officially recorded at 30,000. But estimates reckon that thousands more fans broke into the stadium after the gates were closed. The passionate Middlesbrough supporters, some of whom were even seated around the pitch itself, made the atmosphere feel like a home game. What an enthusiastic following!

At the end of ninety minutes there was still no score, so once again extra-time was played. We were well into the added period, with the players from both sides out on their feet, when our outside-right Johnny Spuhler was brought down inside the Blackpool area.

As captain, I took the responsibility for the resultant penalty kick. Almost before the ball was nestling firmly in the back of the net, the pitch was invaded by our jubilant followers, who carried me shoulder high, off to the dressing-rooms.

The Middlesbrough supporters, and the players, were convinced after we had been victorious in such a titanic struggle, that it was finally going to be our year to lift the cup. But as usual we didn't do ourselves justice. In a total anti-climax, we were beaten on aggregate over two legs in the next round by 1-0 by Bolton Wanderers, and that was the end of our Cup aspirations for another 12 months.

During the first season of peacetime football at Middlesbrough I received a pleasant surprise. A pay rise. The maximum wage was increased to £12 a week. Big money!

The increase was due entirely to efforts of the Players Union which, since its formation in the 1930s, had been striving to secure a decent living wage for footballers.

Although progress was slow with regard to pay and conditions, it was to be the perceived unfairness of the players' contract system which was to later take centre stage. It also threw Middlesbrough FC under the glaring spotlight of national attention and into an acrimonious, and very public, confrontation with one of its star players, the Golden Boy, Wilf Mannion.

There was also a new manager at Ayresome Park, David Jack. He had been appointed in 1944 to replace Wilf Gillow, who had unfortunately died in a Durham hospital following unforeseen complications after a routine operation.

Jack, an international forward of some distinction with England, Bolton and Arsenal, scored over 250 goals during a distinguished career. However he is probably best remembered as the player who, in 1923, struck the very first goal in a Wembley Cup Final. He was a very relaxed character, and because of his personal achievements in the game, he was well respected by all the players.

Middlesbrough at that time was a football club in a period of natural transition. The likes of Wilf Mannion, Mick Fenton and myself had lost a significant part of our official football careers due to the war.

The club also had to compensate for the retirement of their prolific goalscorer, George Camsell, and the transfer of cultured centre-half, Bob Baxter, who had returned to Scotland to play for Hearts.

Even today, along with many of the older supporters with whom I constantly reminisce, I mull over in my mind about the impact Middlesbrough may have made on the First Division in the early 1940s, with a team which was a rich blend of youth and experience. If only our careers had not been interrupted by the conflict with Germany, it might have been so different. On reflection, however, one has to accept that all our lives are littered with many an if only, or a might have been, which we would love to change. In the real world, of course, we never get that opportunity, but it's still pleasant to dream.

Prior to the commencement of the national football league season in 1946/47, David Jack officially awarded me the captaincy of Middlesbrough Football Club. The appointment was a marvellous personal milestone in my professional career.

As a youngster growing up in Lingdale, it had always been my ambition just to play for the Boro, but to be given the opportunity to lead them out was indeed a great honour, and my proud parents were there to watch me do so.

I always took the responsibility of captaincy very seriously. I believe it said something about you as a person, and your ability to mould a squad of individuals, who often varied greatly in temperament, age, ability and background, into a team which could perform to its full potential.

As skipper I was always on call. Off the pitch I was the important link between the management and the players, handing out both criticism and plaudits in equal measure, as and when the need arose.

During a match it was vitally important to know and understand the individual personality of each player before you either harangued, cajoled, or gently encouraged them. A derogatory remark at the wrong time to a sensitive player, could have meant the difference between winning and losing two points.

But above all, captaincy is all about leading by example, setting the tone, gaining respect, and not boring people to death with over long after dinner speeches. Once you have achieved those objectives the job basically boils down to common sense.

Many players have superstitions or routines they perform before a match. For example, always changing in the same place, putting their kit on in a certain order, running out on to the pitch at the end of the line and so on. As captain I often occupied the same position in the dressing room but the only regular routine I tried to continue was to carry a ball out with me on to the pitch. It just felt natural. Whether it was a comforter I don't know, but if I didn't have one with me as I came out of the tunnel I somehow felt undressed. A strange breed, footballers.

At the end of the 1946/47 season the Boro finished a rather unspectacular league campaign in mid-table. It also saw the introduction of David Jack's first signings to replace those players who had either retired or left the club.

The new recruits included Dicky Robinson, Harry Bell, Geoff Walker, Johnny Spuhler and Jimmy Gordon. All of them were to prove excellent buys. They all became fine players and along with Ronnie Dicks, who had joined the club during the war, provided the loyal backbone of the Boro team over the following years.

The final league position of eleventh was also very respectable when taking into consideration that during the course of the season, Wilf and I were frequently called upon to play for England.

In those days there was an unwritten agreement that country came before club and the individuals who were required for representative matches didn't play within seven days of important engagements.

The policy is somewhat different today where the Premier League fixtures are suspended so that internationals can be played. In the 1940s, however, playing for England often coincided with league matches. When that clash occurred the Boro played with an understrength team, and I'm certain it had a negative impact on their overall league position.

The more mature Boro supporter has always believed that our previous ground, Ayresome Park, was stricken with a mystical curse, because while playing there, the club never at any time in their history progressed beyond an FA Cup quarter final.

That statistic was given further credence following the experience of our marathon cup run of 1946/47 when, after defeating Queens Park Rangers and Nottingham Forest in replays, we were drawn against Burnley in the last eight of the competition, at Ayresome Park, in March 1947.

A record crowd of over 52,000 fans somehow shoehorned themselves into the ground and raised the roof when we took the lead with a goal by Geoff Walker. Near the end of normal time, however, a perfectly good goal, scored by Mickey Fenton direct from a free-kick, was disallowed for a dubious offside decision against Johnny Spuhler, who was standing out on the right wing and was harshly adjudged to be interfering with play.

To add insult to injury Burnley, in one of their rare attacks of the second half, broke away to equalise and force an undeserved replay. We certainly felt hard done by, because in the dressing-room discussions after the game we thought we'd done enough to win the tie.

But the disappointment we felt that Saturday afternoon soon paled into insignificance compared with the injustice we suffered three days later in Lancashire.

The circumstances surrounding the outcome of the replay at Turf Moor involved one of the most farcical and bizarre refereeing decisions I witnessed in my entire footballing career.

It started to go wrong immediately after we arrived at the ground from our hotel in Blackpool, on a bitterly cold March afternoon. We observed the Turf Moor groundstaff energetically chipping away at a thick layer of ice on the pitch with pickaxes and large crow bars. Then they proceeded to sprinkle sawdust along the lines in order to make them visible.

After experiencing the Arctic conditions at first hand, none of the Boro lads thought for one moment that the game would go ahead. The referee, Arthur Ellis, who I'd met during the war in the RAF, thought otherwise. After a cursory inspection, Arthur made the amazing decision to declare the rock hard pitch playable.

The concrete surface was quite frankly dangerous and could have caused serious injury to the players. And, although we felt very strongly that the game should have been postponed, we had to abide by his astounding decision.

A game which was of such importance to both teams quickly descended into a comic fiasco as the players skated and slithered on the treacherous underfoot conditions.

The only goal was scored by Burnley in extremely controversial circumstances when, towards the end of extra-time, their left winger Peter Kippax crossed a free-kick into the Boro penalty area. Our goalkeeper, Dave Cumming, saved cleanly enough, but as he landed on the icy surface the ball slithered from his grasp and fell loose.

In the ensuing frantic goalmouth melee, Burnley's Ray Harrison blatantly handled the ball to one of his colleagues, Billy Morris, who proceeded to kick the ball past me into the empty net.

We were all laughing at Harrison's cheek and preparing for a free-kick when to our absolute astonishment the referee awarded the goal. It was totally unbelievable, and no amount of vociferous protests from our players could make him change his mind. In fact Ellis should have sent me off for the steady stream of colourful expletives that flowed in his direction criticising the dreadful decision which allowed the goal to stand.

Unfortunately were out of the Cup, yet again. After that experience even some of the players, who were superstitious at the best of times, began to think that there might well be an element of truth in the notion of an FA Cup curse hanging over Middlesbrough Football Club.

How fitting that Arthur Ellis, who went on to officiate in the 1954 World Cup Final, was later to become a celebrity referee on the BBC's comedy TV gameshow It's a Knockout, hosted by Stuart Hall and Eddie Waring, because his decision that wintery day was certainly a case of playing his joker.

The 1947/48 league campaign was a season of great highs and lows. We finally finished in a very mediocre 16th position, winning only one of our last dozen or so matches.

The playing staff had been strengthened with the purchase from Chesterfield of centre-half Bill Whitaker, who can only be described as a genuinely nice man, Jimmy McCormack from Gateshead, and a goalkeeper from Sheffield Wednesday, Derek Goodfellow.

What a character our new custodian turned out to be. Derek, who had been a marine commando during the war years, was as hard as nails and became involved in two memorable incidents which are worthy of a reprise.

The first occurred during a league game at Maine Road, Manchester, when City's burly centre-forward, Eddie McMorran, spent the whole game constantly impeding Derek. Unfortunately he did it once too often. Goodfellow, having been fouled to the ground for the umpteenth time, quickly jumped to his feet and with one hand, screwed the front of Eddie McMorran's jersey tightly together under his chin.

He then proceeded to lift the choking forward into the air, carried him slowly to the penalty spot, and advised the City striker not to come any closer to his goal than that, if he valued his life.

The referee quite sensibly, in my view, remained an interested observer while the little *tête-a-tête* ran its course and Derek made his valid point.

Surprisingly, for the rest of the match, even though we did eventually lose 2-0, nobody went anywhere near him.

The second incident involving Big Derek occurred during a mid-season training break in Scarborough.

On our one free night, most of the lads had been to the cinema and then moved on to a local hostelry for a few libations, before returning to our base, the Pavilion Hotel.

While we were having a drink in the pub, Eddie Murphy, who during the war had been in the Royal Navy, uttered the disparaging expression, "Wardroom Flunkeys", which was frequently used by navy men to describe the marines.

To say that Derek Goodfellow was not best pleased with the remark would be an understatement, and if the 5'4" inside-forward had not been so nimble on his feet, he would have been torn apart limb by limb, and then hung out to dry.

Unfortunately for Eddie, he was only delaying the inevitable, because he'd forgotten he was sharing a room with the ex-marine.

A few minutes after we arrived back at the Pavilion, we were soon alerted by one hell of a commotion coming from the top floor of the hotel. We all flew upstairs to locate the source of the problem, and established that the din was emanating from behind Eddie and Derek's locked bedroom door.

Fearing we may have a possible fatality on our hands, I dispatched one of the lads to quickly nip downstairs and borrow the hall porter's master key from reception.

Bursting into the room we found poor little Eddie being dangled out of the window, some three storeys above the ground, with an irate Big Derek bellowing out his demands for an immediate apology.

At our insistence, Eddie duly apologised for his comment and was hauled back into the relative safety of the room, looking decidedly wan and shaky from his high rise experience.

Despite the initial seriousness of the situation, when tempers eventually calmed down, it was difficult not to see the funny side of the episode. However, for Eddie Murphy, it had been a hard lesson in keeping a civil tongue in your head.

The season's highlights on the pitch were mainly dominated by the glorious month of November, when we won four games in a row, scoring twenty goals into the bargain, and a bizarre away defeat by Arsenal, at Highbury, in March.

The home game against Blackpool in the autumn of 1947 has become woven into the rich tapestry of Ayresome Park folklore and mythology, and is simply known by the fans as the Mannion Match.

Much has been written about Wilf's sublime individual performance in front of his fiance Bernadette that day, in our resounding 4-0 victory. I can only concur with the complimentary comments made in the press and by supporters at the time, and since. By any standards it was a virtuoso display. Wilf performed an expert demonstration of his innate footballing talents, and engaged in some outrageous individual party pieces, such as juggling the ball on his head as he was running.

None of the Boro players were aware of the motive behind Wilf's exhibition that afternoon, but during the private inquisitions that followed in the dressing room after the game, some questions were asked as to why he didn't strive to attain that level of performance in every league match.

For our next fixture we travelled to Ewood Park to play Blackburn Rovers with the press comments about Wilf's display against Blackpool still making good copy. To their credit the other players also raised their game, and we gave one of the most outstanding and fluent away performances under my Boro captaincy, with Jimmy McCormack grabbing a hat-trick. We eventually ran out comfortable winners by 7-1, scoring four goals in the last ten minutes, and even had two efforts disallowed. The margin of our victory was so comprehensive that by the end of the match the Rovers supporters were generously applauding our play.

As a reward for our autumnal efforts, we were given a five day mid-season break in Scarborough, where we spent the time training, relaxing, playing golf and dangling our fellow professionals out of hotel windows.

I remember the game at Highbury against Arsenal so vividly because it featured the one and only fleeting appearance made for Middlesbrough by a young goalkeeper called Bobbie Anderson. What a nightmare it was for the poor inexperienced lad. His performance was littered with elementary handling errors, as we finished up on the wrong end of a 7-0 drubbing. And unfortunately he was at fault for most of them.

I don't know if he was overcome by a severe case of debutant nerves, but his afternoon was made complete when we were awarded a free-kick for offside, just on the edge of our penalty area.

As Bobbie was about to take the free-kick the Arsenal forward, Ronnie Rooks, was ambling towards the halfway line with his back to our goal. Unfortunately his attempted clearance, which was well hit, but low, struck Rooks hard on the shoulder. The ball then flew high into the air, arching beautifully over the young keeper's disbelieving head, before dropping softly into our net.

Poor Bobbie never played again for Middlesbrough, after conceding one of the most bizarre goals I've ever had the dubious privilege of observing on a football field. He eventually moved into local league football with Blackhall Colliery Welfare at the end of the season.

A confounded knee ligament injury sustained in April during the England v Scotland game ruined my summer break which I usually spent between playing cricket for Normanby Hall and coaching on the FA's close season training courses.

Instead of relaxing, I was a permanent fixture in the Ayresome Park treatment room, keeping our conscientious trainer Tommy Mayson company. To be fair, Tommy did a wonderful job, and I was ready to return to action before the new, and highly controversial, season got under way.

The beginning of the 1948/49 campaign found Wilf Mannion at loggerheads with the club after his formal request for a transfer was denied. Wilf was so annoyed by the club's intransigence, that he effectively went on strike. He refused to play for Middlesbrough, and to all intents and purposes, withdrew his labour.

I knew exactly what was on Wilf's mind. Both he and I had frequently been offered very large tax free sums of money by interested third parties if we could arrange to have our names placed on the transfer list. We both knew that there was a great deal of money to be earned elsewhere from our football talents if we could get a move away from Teesside.

I was even approached on the platform of King's Cross station, while waiting to board a train for home after an international game, and offered £4,000 in the proverbial brown envelope to engineer such a move. It was a tremendous amount of money in those days. But I tactfully declined the invitation. It was something to do with that abstract feeling called a conscience.

While I was away on international duty, I also heard from other established England players how much they were earning from various outside business interests, sanctioned by their clubs, to keep them sweet.

At Ayresome Park the situation was totally different. The players, it has to be strongly emphasised, received everything to which they were entitled, but no more.

The club was noted for always being run on very tight financial lines with Herbert Glasper renowned for exercising monetary prudence. Our change strip was so old that the navy blue shorts were washed out, and it looked as though we played in all white kit away from home. Also, after training, the bath water was usually stone cold in order to save on the heating bills, and if you dared to ask for another piece of wafer thin soda soap, trainer Charlie Cole's retort was always: "What do you think we're running here, a millionaire's club?"

I certainly feel that this extremely frugal state of affairs rankled Wilf, who believed he was being undervalued. So, consequently, at the start of the season, the Golden Boy was determined to make a stand.

As the impasse dragged on for months, with claim and counter claim, attitudes on both sides became more entrenched.

With no source of income, Wilf accepted the offer of work from an Oldham businessman and eventually moved to Lancashire, where he lived in self-imposed exile.

At the time much was written about the situation. And even today, post-Bosman, the episode has been repeatedly reviewed. There has been wholesale questioning of the moral legitimacy of the professional contract system and how, 50 years ago, it bordered on football slavery.

In those days, when you signed for a football club, as I did at the age of seventeen, you had no legal representation, and were totally oblivious as to the long term consequences of your action. For most teenagers in the 1930s, becoming a footballer was the ultimate ambition, providing an escape route from the prevailing economic climate.

To be fair, the vagaries of the contract system would never become an issue for the vast majority of solid journeymen players, who were bought and sold without any problems. It did, however, undoubtedly affect the rights of the star players, and Wilf's challenge to the rigid system became a test case.

Essentially, the whole Wilf Mannion Saga was about money, security and the right to sell your talents to the highest bidder. In other words, the employment principles adopted by any other profession.

Wilf was without question one of the greatest talents in the game at that time, and he was arguing for the right to capitalise on his notoriety.

The stand-off developed into a very messy episode in the history of Middlesbrough FC and one which certain club officials would never forgive or forget.

Keeping Wilf Mannion at Ayresome Park became a battle of wills, which in the long run, benefitted neither.party. And for those people searching for a reason as to why Wilf was never granted an official testimonial by the club until 1983, you need look no further for your answer.

Wilf dared to challenge the status quo, and although it was never admitted in public by the club, he was made to suffer the consequences.

What I personally never fully understood about the whole situation was that if open cheque books were being waved, and record offers in excess of £30,000 were received for Wilf's services from other clubs, why didn't the directors just cut their losses, swallow their pride, and accept the money? Speaking from a Boro player's point of view, Wilf's heart, quite understandably, was never in the club when he was forced to eat humble pie and return to Ayresome Park in the New Year.

The rest of the players tried to carry on as normal, but with both the local and national press detailing every move of Wilf's stand, we struggled through the first half of the season and found goals particularly hard to come by.

When Wilf finally returned to the club in the January he was patently unfit and clearly unhappy with his predicament. I was personally glad he'd returned to the fold, and went on the record at the time as saying so. However, rightly or wrongly, there was still a lot of bad feeling in certain areas. Behind the scenes I had to build a few dressing-room bridges. Some of the players, with lesser abilities than Wilf's, felt that they had been let down. They did not appreciate why Wilf had taken the stance that he did.

However the main thing on my mind was that it was imperative that the club forgot about the political in-fighting that was tarnishing its image, and concentrated on preserving its First

Division status. We needed everybody to pull together. It is fair to say that the episode had greatly affected our season. We were fighting for our lives and battling to keep the club out of the Second Division.

It was no surprise that the 1949 relegation dog-fight went right down to the wire. In the event we needed to take the minimum of one point from our final match of the season at Villa Park to avoid the dreaded drop.

Before the game, which was one of my most important for Middlesbrough, I received hundreds of Good Luck telegrams in the dressing-room. It was clear that a lot of people were willing us to stay up. One message in particular, from Dorman Long Engineering, summed up the mood in the town perfectly and read: "This company expects every man to do his duty."

I'm glad to say we did. It wasn't the most attractive team performance I'd ever been involved in, but my goodness what a battle we put up that afternoon. We rolled up our sleeves and fought like tigers for every ball. We took a first half lead, courtesy of an Andy Donaldson fluke goal, which inadvertently went into the net off his shins.

However, Andy's goal was all that we needed to increase our resolution to hang on to our First Division status. We then defended our advantage with stubborn determination until Villa equalised ten minutes from time.

The home side then laid siege to our goal. I don't think I've ever wasted so much time as I did in that nerve-jangling finale as Villa powered forward in the hope of winning the game. The ball seemed to spend as much time kicked high into the stands as it did on the pitch. The referee's whistle came finally as a blessed relief, and signalled our top flight survival. There were some celebrations in the dressing-room afterwards which couldn't have been any better if we had won the Championship.

Another lasting personal memory of that season was scoring two penalties to win the local derby 3-2 against Newcastle.

Many of the supporters who attended that game said I looked calm and collected, but I can assure them as I walked back to take the first of those penalties I was a very worried man.

Being Easter, it was my third game in four days and I was

struggling with constant pain in my left knee. So, in order not to aggravate it any further, I was favouring my right foot as much as possible.

In normal circumstances, because I was carrying an injury, I would have asked for volunteers to take a penalty. But as we were losing 1-0, and there was so much at stake in our fight against relegation, I decided to take the responsibility myself.

After I'd placed the ball on the spot and turned away to start my run up, all sorts of questions were flashing through my mind. Should I take it with my right foot? Will I be able to strike it hard enough with my left? What will happen if my knee gives way altogether?

Eventually, after what seemed an age, but in reality was only a few seconds, I decided to risk my left foot.

Once I'd made that decision I focused all my concentration on to the back of the ball, and nothing else. Then, after choosing my corner I shot as hard as I could.

The relief which followed was not the result of me scoring, but the fact that my knee had held up. So when we were awarded a second penalty I had the confidence to step up and score again, which secured a derby victory over our North-eastern neighbours. But more importantly it earned us two vital points in our fight against the drop.

Two significant new faces were also introduced into the dressing-room that season. One was the extrovert goalkeeper Rolando Ugolini, who joined us from Celtic.

Ugo, as he affectionately became known, was full of mischief and turned out to be a fine shot stopper, going on to eventually play over 300 games for the club.

The second new player was Alex McCrae, who signed from Charlton Athletic. Alex was a very underrated player. He possessed great control and always gave us an extra option, because he had the uncanny knack of finding space in which to receive the ball. This ability often helped to relieve the pressure on our defence.

As usual, during the close season, I worked for the FA on a variety of summer training courses. Football coaching was now to play an increasingly important role in my future because, following a knee injury, I had failed to regain my place in the

England side. As a result, my international career appeared to be over.

The 1949/50 season showed a great improvement in the team's overall performance. Wilf was back in the fold, and with the new forward partnership of Peter McKennan, who was signed from Brentford, and Alex McCrae, we posed much more of an attacking threat to the opposition.

Outside of football I'd taken over as manager of a newly opened sports shop on Linthorpe Road, in Middlesbrough. Although at the time the appointment took second place to my football career, it was a business venture which I thought may have some benefit for the future.

The season's highlight was again undoubtedly the derby match against Newcastle United, which created a new ground attendance record for Ayresome Park of nearly 54,000.

We had beaten the Geordies the day before, on Boxing Day, with a goal from Alex McCrae, so there was a great deal of interest in the return fixture from the fervent Teesside fans twenty-four hours later.

The atmosphere for the match, to use a cliche, was electric. Sitting in the dressing-rooms at Ayresome Park before important games, you could always feel the air of expectancy and anticipation created by a big attendance. It helped to keep the adrenaline flowing freely for both sets of players.

The crowd on that day, particularly in the Bob End, was just a huge sea of faces which swayed from side to side as they followed the action. In fact, there were so many people in the ground that young children were passed down to the front of the terraces, above the heads of the fans, to watch the match in safety on the cinder track.

In a closely fought game, Peter McKennan scored the only goal, enabling us to complete a famous 48 hour double over The Magpies.

The match was unfortunately missed by one of our most avid supporters, the Evening Gazette sports writer, Cliff Mitchell, who had been rushed into Newcastle General Hospital the previous day for an emergency operation on a perforated ulcer, after being taken seriously ill at St James' Park.

It was somewhat ironic, that in a long and very distinguished career spanning nearly forty years in local newspapers, Cliff should miss the game which recorded the largest all time attendance at Ayresome Park. But I'm sure our victory helped his speedy recovery.

During my career I had a fine working relationship with the local press, firstly with J.W. Bavin, better known as Captain Jack, and then with Cliff Mitchell. Both correspondents were gentleman and good friends. They endeavoured to always report the facts with an honesty and integrity which seems sadly lacking in today's search for the sensational tabloid headline.

In January, I tore my rib muscles so badly in an FA Cup replay at Ayresome Park against Aston Villa, that I played in only two more league matches during that campaign. Tommy Blenkinsopp and George Hepple ably covered my absence.

The FA Cup tie spanned three matches and, during the third and decisive match held at Elland Road, which we won 3-0, I saw one of the greatest goals ever scored by a Boro player. It was Alex McCrae who picked up a clearance in the Boro half and swerved his way past three Villa defenders. Then, from outside the area, he hit a tremendous shot past the stunned Villa keeper for a truly memorable strike.

Once again, however, with Wembley calling, we contrived to lose in the next round, by 3-2 at Second Division Chesterfield. It was a bad defeat and was the result of a poor performance. Unfortunately it seemed to be par for the course for Middlesbrough as the Cup dream ended for yet another year.

After recovering from my muscle injury I returned to play in a match away at Chelsea over Easter which was headlined in the press as The Battle of Stamford Bridge.

It wasn't a particularly physical game, but I can never remember a team receiving so many injuries as Middlesbrough did that afternoon. We finished the match with only seven fit players, and most of those were walking wounded.

There were no substitutes in those days and when our centre-forward Peter McKennan broke his knee cap in the first half and then, disgracefully, had to wait ten minutes for a stretcher to remove him from the pitch, the omens were not good. Other players also received heavy knocks which required attention, before our full-back, Tommy Blenkinsopp, proceeded to pull a thigh muscle so badly that he became a passenger out on the wing. Unfortunately, during all the medical mayhem, Chelsea took the lead.

At half-time, rather than feeling sorry for ourselves, there was a mood of determination in the dressing-room to overcome the injury crisis. And immediately after the restart our positive intentions were rewarded when Wilf scored a fine equaliser.

For the rest of the game we defended doggedly, with Bill Whitaker outstanding at centre-half and Wilf constantly retaining possession, we managed to absorb the mounting pressure.

Then about ten minutes from time I wrenched my knee and, although I tried to carry on, I had to leave the field. The lads just could not hold out in a hectic finale and Chelsea scored to deny us the draw our fighting spirit had so richly deserved.

In football it is often said, you only get out of the game what you put in. Well I can assure you the effort put in by those players representing Middlesbrough FC that afternoon went totally unrewarded. It was a fully committed all-round team performance and I was proud to be associated with such a sterling display.

It was at that juncture in my career that I had to be honest with myself and plan for the future. I realised because of the deterioration in my knee's condition, that I would be unable to play in the First Division for much longer. Playing at that level week in and week out required a high standard of fitness, and I knew that I would find it increasingly difficult to do myself justice.

Until then I had been able to cope at that level because of my ability to read the game. But I did not want to suffer the indignity of being a passenger in the team or become, as I had seen with other mature professionals, a player who was living off his past reputation.

I therefore made the conscious decision to look for another challenge. One which would allow me to pursue my keen interest in coaching. We didn't have agents in those days to pass the word around the soccer grapevine. But It wasn't long before I was receiving my first job offers from abroad.

In July 1950 a very pleasant letter arrived from the secretary of Hamrun Spartans. Mr Antonio Pellegrini was offering me of a position to coach the Maltese club's young team, who he believed would be successful under my "expert" guidance. The potential salary was good and the prospect of coaching abroad was very attractive. I'm sure that I could have done a good job for the Spartans. But I had my wife Joy and son Mike to consider, so I politely declined the position.

The interest from Malta did prove to me, however, that the word about Hardwick's coaching ability was spreading. Sooner rather than later I felt that other more tempting job offers would come my way.

Middlesbrough started the 1950/51 campaign very well. In fact at one stage we headed the First Division table.

Football's bush telegraph had also gone into overdrive during the summer and I was beginning to receive solid offers from other English clubs for my services. For example Everton wanted me as their player/coach, though Middlesbrough were not keen to release me at the time and the possibility of moving to Goodison Park never got off the ground.

It had always been my intention to move into management, which would enable me to fully develop my coaching ability and also exercise control over team affairs. So when, in the autumn of 1950, Oldham Athletic offered me a position as their player/manager I felt it was just too good an opportunity to ignore.

That decision was to be the watershed of my footballing career.

I have often been asked whether it was a wrench to leave Ayresome Park and the only club I'd really wanted to play for. The answer to that question is a resounding Yes.

However, as it was my own personal decision to leave Middlesbrough and they did not dispense with my services, I had no regrets about moving to Oldham and beginning a new chapter of my football career.

I realised I couldn't play in top flight any more and therefore I felt it was the correct career decision to make at the time.

So after ending a thirteen year association with my hometown club, I headed west for Lancashire, and the unknown territory of the Third Division North.

As with most things in my life, as one door closed another opened, and I was certainly looking forward to the challenge at Boundary Park.

• SIX •

England – My halcyon years

The resumption of official international matches in 1946 led to the Football Association once again awarding full caps to the players.

Those individuals who had represented England during the war, and in the Victory internationals, received a decorative handwritten scroll listing their appearances, signed by the FA executive acknowledging their selection.

In some ways I preferred having my achievements detailed in neat calligraphy. Once it was framed and hung on the wall, it became a concise visual reminder of the wartime games in which I played.

There were other changes taking place on the international scene. The same year, after a long personal campaign by FA secretary, Stanley Rous, England appointed Walter Winterbottom as their first manager and director of coaching. In many respects it was quite a revolutionary move.

Walter, who had trained as a schoolteacher at Chester and Carnegie College in Leeds, was a more than useful half-back in the late 1930s with Manchester United.

During the war he'd attained the influential rank of Wing Commander and had co-ordinated the Air Ministry's physical training programme. He'd also guested with me for Chelsea, before persistent back trouble prematurely ended his playing career.

Stanley Rous, who has to be acknowledged as a rare breed, a football administrator with vision, was convinced that the FA needed an expert coach on its staff to oversee the movement towards a greater technical appreciation of the game.

The idea of a supremo being appointed initially received a frosty reception from the staid FA Council members. But their objections soon subsided when, surprise surprise, they realised Winterbottom would be undertaking two jobs for the price of one salary.

I have to say I agreed with many of Walter's innovative proposals. They began with the appointment of a nationwide network of coaches including Joe Mercer, Matt Busby and myself.

From our base at Bisham Abbey the brief was to devise a national strategy which would develop the technical aspects of the game at grass root level through the school and district associations. Later, that blueprint developed into a framework of county youth championships, international youth tournaments and the prestigious FA Youth Cup.

Walter Winterbottom was an unassuming and thorough man who thought deeply about the game. He did not consciously seek publicity and tended to keep a low profile. Few people outside the football fraternity fully appreciated his tremendous capacity for work. To the detriment of his family life, he travelled thousands of miles over the years organising courses for managers, coaches, teachers, referees and youth leaders to ensure the game's countrywide development and appeal.

Although there have been many long running debates as to the value of football coaching, I firmly believed then, and still do now, that a good coach can make a positive contribution to improving the quality of both individual and team performances.

However, I do agree with those purists who say that outstanding players like Tom Finney, George Best and Michael Owen are born and not made. No amount of coaching can manufacture that sort of greatness because it is simply innate. But by the same token I also believe that sound qualified coaching harnesses, develops, and nurtures natural talent so it can realise its potential. Possessing talent is one thing, but knowing how to apply it effectively is another. Acquiring that understanding is right at the heart of my own personal coaching philosophy.

Dedication is another vital ingredient for success. From an early age I was a football fanatic and had an inner determination to do the most with my limited ability.

In the 1930s achieving your ambition was the result of many hours of hard work spent practising your skills. If you realised your aspirations you made damn sure, injuries permitting, that you stayed at the top for as long as possible.

What saddens me today is that the words dedication and loyalty seem too unfashionable for the contemporary game, where endorsed boots are for hire to the highest bidder.

Playing football is a privileged lifestyle and it should never be taken for granted.

Even if I do say it myself, one of my main personal attributes is that I have an ability to communicate with people. I enjoy company. It was for that reason, coupled with my love for the great game of football, that I decided to become an FA coach.

After the war I started coaching youngsters on schemes financed by the local North-Eastern Weekly News and the North Riding Education Committee. We used venues all across Teesside including Arthur Head School in Stockton, Priory Hall, Guisborough, Sandsend Institute and my former school in Lingdale. It was an experience I really enjoyed and I was ably assisted by my Boro team-mate Mick Fenton.

Although these very successful demonstration sessions were mainly held in school halls, I was able to make close contact with the next generation of footballers, which I felt was important for the local development of the game.

So, once I'd finished training with Middlesbrough I would spend most of my afternoons and evenings coaching. I was willing and keen and found I could relate to the kids. They in turn attended the sessions in their hundreds.

It was through the coaching scheme that I first met Keith Schellenburg, who represented Great Britain at the Winter Olympics in the bobsleigh. He approached me with the splendid idea of forming a local Youth Club Charity Association which would organise and promote events to raise funds for the youngsters of Teesside. We were supported in our venture by Lady Crathorne and such was the success of the scheme that, over a five year period, we raised a considerable amount of money for the project.

On the strength of the coaching courses' popularity I was asked, in August 1947, to write a weekly series of articles on football skills which appeared in Kemsley Newspapers' North-Eastern Weekly News. And over the next forty years I was gainfully associated with both the local and national press, who were keen to print my sometimes forthright and outspoken opinions on the burning football issues of the day.

After the Second World War, as I began to build a reputation as a technician and tutor of some ability, I was invited to coach on the official FA courses at Scarborough and Carnegie College in Leeds. Later in the 1950s, along with Joe Mercer, I coached the England youth team at Bisham Abbey. A number of the young players in my charge became some of the all-time greats of English football, including Jimmy Greaves, Duncan Edwards and Bobby Charlton.

Most of the those lads came for a summer training camp. And as well as football coaching they received lessons in basic social skills, such as table etiquette, which prepared them to represent their country at formal functions at home and aboard.

In those days, how you conducted yourself both on and off the field was very important. There was a time if you were booked while playing for England, your place would be in serious jeopardy. The FA took a very dim view of any misdemeanour. Sadly the same standards do not seem to apply today. Money dominates the game. Clubs play to win, sometimes at all costs, and players' indiscretions appear to be an acceptable and "colourful" part of football.

I was only ever sent off once in the whole of my playing career when I was player/manager of Oldham Athletic. Even now thinking about the incident makes me angry. I'm still convinced it was a case of mistaken identity. But you can judge for yourself when the episode is discussed more fully in a later chapter.

In 1946 the newly created position of England manager was plagued by constant outside interference. The team was still chosen by a stuffy committee of club representatives who tended to favour certain players and would not be hurried into changing their traditional selection procedure.

During the early part of his tenure, Walter Winterbottom employed no great tactical system, preferring to rely totally on the instinctive spontaneity of the plethora of gifted players available for selection. And he really was spoilt for choice.

His rather earnest, prep school style of management and training methods were, however, treated with deep suspicion by some of the senior players who were uneasy with the new technical jargon.

Rough diamond Raich Carter in particular was not afraid to ask what was the "effing point" prior to some of the basic practice routines in which he was asked to participate.

After the war, the presentation and image of the national team suddenly became very important factors to the administrators. And when blazers were introduced for players on England duty, there were again rumblings of discontent among some of the more senior squad members that we were being asked to dress up like public schoolboys.

I personally had no problem with the blazers because they identified you as an England footballer. I was proud to represent my country and I wanted everybody else to know it.

Despite the initial criticism of his methods, Walter Winterbottom must have been doing something right because he held this country's most prestigious football management position for over 15 years before stepping down.

I also feel that his successor, Alf Ramsey, certainly benefitted from Walter's endeavours. In my opinion he laid the foundations of our success in winning the 1966 World Cup.

In fact I would go as far as to say that Winterbottom did more to improve the standard of football coaching in this country than any man I have ever known. And I feel that is a fact which has never been widely acknowledged within the game.

The first England get-together under the stewardship of Winterbottom was held at the Buxton Spa Hotel prior to a match against Scotland at Maine Road, Manchester, which had been organised in aid of the Bolton Disaster Fund.

The tragedy had occurred at Burnden Park in March, when the sheer weight of numbers trying to attend Bolton's FA Cup match with Stoke, in which Stan Matthews was playing, caused the barriers to collapse at the railway embankment end of the ground. It resulted in 33 spectators being crushed to death and shocked football people the length and breadth of the country.

The game to raise money for the appeal was no exhibition match. In fact it was a real battle, ending in a 2-2 draw, with me sporting a black eye and torn shorts.

I was, however, generally pleased with my overall performance, as were some of the reporters present who noted:

"There was no better back on the field than Hardwick who, despite two injuries in the second half, played with the heart of a lion and tackled the best wing afield in courageous fashion."

The relaxed stay in rural Derbyshire did much to allay the initial suspicion about the new manager's coaching methods and also helped to foster a positive team spirit which was carried forward into a very successful international season.

In September 1946, the squad to play games against Northern Ireland and Eire was announced. Those fixtures would be very significant because they were the first official full England international matches played in the post war era.

They were also of considerable personal significance because I had the honour of being elected, by FA committee vote, the captain of my country. That initial appointment led to 13 continuous international appearances as captain. In all of those matches we only lost once, away to Switzerland, when we did everything but score.

I have often been asked how I was informed about the England captaincy. Well to be honest it was completely unexpected and done in accordance with the rather formal FA procedures of that time. I received the notification of my election in an official letter delivered to my home in Saltburn. And unlike the newly appointed contemporary captains, who are paraded in front of the full glare of a media circus, often to the accompaniment of great musical fanfares, it was a very low key affair. That, however, did not detract from the fact that I was still an immensely proud man to have been chosen to lead my country.

As England captain I forged a good relationship with the manager Walter Winterbottom. As I've stated previously, I admired his coaching methods and during a contemporary radio broadcast, discussing football from that era, he was kind enough to pay me this very complimentary tribute:

"George was a typical example of the English full-back of the day, strong in the tackle, quick on his feet, a good header of the ball with the ability to hit the long ball pass down the wing or through the centre. Above all he was a fine man who had a clean cut well groomed image, possessed great leadership qualities, and was a good communicator both on and off the field. He rarely said anything against referees and when the need arose he was a good public speaker at formal occasions. All the players respected him as a fine leader and that was good enough for me."

The relationship between the football manager and his team captain cannot be underestimated. They need to work in tandem and my rapport with Walter was very constructive indeed.

I found him to be approachable and, being an ex-professional, he had my respect because he understood the vagaries of the game.

Once we were out on the pitch, however, I was in total charge of the team, and by using a combination of my perceptive man management skills and forceful personality, I was able encourage the players to perform to the best of their ability.

I also believe that full-back is a good position from which to captain a side, because it gives you an overall perspective of a match, enabling you to tactically control the game and provide your team-mates with constructive assistance.

The England team which I was so proud to lead in the late 1940s contained, in my opinion, some of the greatest players of all time including:

Tom Finney (Preston NE), Stanley Matthews (Blackpool), Laurie Scott (Arsenal), Tommy Lawton (Chelsea), Stan Mortensen (Blackpool), Frank Swift (Manchester City), Neil Franklin (Stoke City), Raich Carter (Derby County), Wilf Mannion (Middlesbrough), Bobby Langton (Blackburn Rovers) and Billy Wright (Wolverhampton Wanderers).

Most of us had played together in the forces, and that experience helped to develop a tremendous team spirit and an almost telepathic understanding of each other's game. We were a side that possessed an abundance of individual talent and a belief in our collective ability. Not to put too finer point on it, we simply thought we were better than any of the opposition.

Our headquarters prior to the matches in Ireland was the Slieve Donard Hotel which was situated in the lovely countryside surrounding, Newcastle, County Down.

It had marvellous facilities for golf and pool, the American form of snooker, at which Tommy Lawton, Raich Carter and Wilf Mannion became quite proficient. In other words they hustled money from their team-mates.

The scenery in Ireland was stunningly beautiful and the people so warm and welcoming. I made many friends and contacts and later returned to play in numerous charity and exhibition matches and did some coaching for the FA of Eire in the 1950s.

The match against Northern Ireland was played at Windsor Park, Belfast, home of Linfield Football Club. It created so much interest that at one stage the game was in doubt because there were nearly 60,000 people trying to get into the ground and they spilled over onto the playing area. We were changed and ready to take the field when the referee, Willie Webb, came into our dressing room and told me not to lead the lads out until he gave the all clear. It was only after numerous persuasive announcements and appeals over the tannoy were made for the supporters to retreat back over the barriers that the match started about a quarter of an hour late.

The game itself turned out to be something of an exhibition, with England running out comfortable winners by 7-2. Wilf in particular was in great form, scoring two goals and entertaining the crowd with his dribbling ability. Another to catch the eye was Tom Finney, who had an impressive debut on the right-wing.

The following morning we travelled on to Dublin, and during the course of our stay in that very atmospheric city, we were taken to Government House to meet Eire's Taoiseach, the charismatic Eamon de Valera. That was an historic meeting because it was the first occasion in which de Valera had agreed to meet the members of a "foreign" football team.

During the formal photo call, to record the meeting for posterity, we all found him to be very personable. He chatted freely with us before concluding with the hope that the game against Eire would not be as easy as the previous Saturday in Belfast.

The hope of the Irish Premier was certainly realised in the match played in front of 32,000 of his partisan countryman at Dalymount Park, Dublin. The Eire team played with great spirit and determination, adhering strictly to a set game plan. Their constant spoiling tactics paid dividends, but they were helped in no small measure by a heavy pitch and strong wind, which went some way to negating our superior skill. We were very fortunate to win the match 1-0 with a goal, rather against the run of play, from Tom Finney.

Being under pressure and having to defend for long periods meant I was always in the thick of the action. In fact I would put that match down as one of my best defensive displays for England. It was an opinion which was endorsed by our goalkeeper big Frank Swift, who gave me a congratulatory pat on the back for my endeavours at the final whistle.

My great friend Johnny Carey, the captain of Eire that afternoon, also had a tremendous game and on reflection he didn't deserve to be on the losing side.

The Eire FA were, as usual, overwhelming in their hospitality towards the England team, and the after match banquet at the Gresham Hotel must rank as one of the best I ever attended in the whole of my international career.

An added bonus of the trip was that we were able to buy numerous items which were still strictly rationed after the war in Britain. Many of us again took the opportunity to buy food and clothing for our families, so it turned out to be a productive excursion all round.

As a result of our battling performance against the Irish, the selection committee chose the same team to play Wales in October 1946 in Manchester. However, as I recall, there was some controversy in the press that Stan Matthews, available again after injury, had not been restored to the side.

We reported two days before the game to a hotel in Southport which had been a lucky omen for Frank Swift because it was apparently where Manchester City had stayed prior to heading south and their FA Cup triumph of 1934.

The match, at Maine Road, was totally dominated by England and we ran out comfortable 3-0 winners with Wilf again in fine form, scoring two of the goals.

A fortnight later we met Holland at Leeds Road, Huddersfield, and had a thumping 8-2 victory over the unfortunate part-time Dutchmen, with Tommy Lawton producing an outstanding display at centre-forward.

But the lasting memory most of the players have of that game was the coach journey from the Majestic Hotel in Harrogate to the Leeds Road ground. I'm sure the driver thought he was participating in a Formula One Grand Prix because we travelled at such breakneck speed that one of the lads remarked out loud: "Hey mate, where's the fire?"

And I swear we took some of the corners on two wheels. How we arrived at the ground in one piece I'll never know.

At the post match banquet in Harrogate, there was a very poignant speech made by the President of the Dutch FA, Karel Lotsy, who had been a member of the underground movement in the Netherlands during the war.

In a deeply moving tribute, and in a voice often breaking with emotion, he thanked the people of Britain for all the help they had given his fellow Dutchmen during the enormous hardship they'd suffered under German occupation.

Over a decade later, Karel Lotsy was to be primarily responsible for my appointment as chief coach to the Dutch national side.

To emerge from that long tunnel into the deafening Wembley amphitheatre, the spiritual home of football, leading your country's national team, has to be one of the proudest moments in any footballer's career.

Unfortunately, I was to experience that sensation only once in April 1947, against Scotland.

The game from an England point of view was a total disappointment, ending in a 1-1 draw. All credit, however, must be given to Scotland because they raised their game that afternoon, and after taking the lead through McClaren on the quarter hour, they managed to subdue the wing play of Stan Matthews with a determined and well-organised defence.

We eventually equalised early in the second half through Raich Carter and, although our overall lacklustre performance certainly didn't merit a victory, we were denied a win with a strange mix-up over an offside decision.

The confusion began as Tommy Lawton slid the ball through to Raich Carter who had a clear run on goal. But a muddled combination of a linesman's frantic flag waving and a French referee's theatrical hand signalling caused the game to stop momentarily.

As the Scottish defenders stood like statues, Carter realised that no offside decision had been given and went on to shoot straight at their goalkeeper, Miller. In all honesty if Raich had scored, the result would have been an total injustice, because for long periods of the game we were completely outplayed.

One of the perks of being England captain, and an international footballer, was that after matches the team would socialise together, particularly in the fashionable London night spots where we were often treated like modern day pop stars.

Young women were attracted to us in droves and there were many opportunities for fraternisation.

We also met celebrities from other walks of life. Most of the time these meetings were rather contrived for the convenience of the press and profit conscious box-office managers who were keen to have their forthcoming attractions photographed with the well-known England players.

At one such photographic session we were introduced to the top American boxer, Joe Baxi, who came to visit us while we were training down in Brighton for an international game.

Baxi, who was in England to fight British heavyweight hope Bruce Woodcock at Harringay, performed a few, gentle exercises, for the benefit of the assembled snappers and then suggested he sparred with a volunteer for affect. Although I'd done some boxing in the RAF, there was no way, even as captain, I was going to respond to that request. In the end Frank Swift, who was taller and had hands which were much bigger than Baxi's, participated in a harmless exhibition of shadow boxing to placate the press, while the rest of the England team watched on from a safe distance.

Baxi's extra training stint with us must have given him the vital edge he needed because he despatched Woodcock, watched by some of the players who'd been given complimentary tickets, inside seven rounds.

After the disappointing draw against the Scots at Wembley, we had the opportunity three weeks later in May, to quickly redeem ourselves, particularly in the eyes of the footballing press who had openly criticised our uninspiring performance. This time the opposition was France and the game was played at Arsenal's Highbury Stadium.

It was a very physical game, as I recall, with the French doing their utmost to stifle the superior skill of Wilf Mannion and Tom Finney.

The Belgian referee's interpretation of the laws of the game left a lot to be desired. We had to endure some intimidating tactics, such as blatant body checking and obstruction, a good deal of which went unpunished and introduced an element of needle into the game.

In front of a crowd of over 50,000 we failed to break down their determined combative resistance before half-time, but that was partly due to Tommy Lawton leaving the field for a significant period to receive treatment on a deep cut after a clash of heads.

Wilf again did much to change the course of the match in the second half by quickly crafting on a goal for Tom Finney, and then scoring one himself, before Raich Carter secured us a comfortable victory ten minutes from the end.

The following week I had the honour of being selected for Great Britain to play in a unique footballing occasion against the Rest of Europe at Hampden Park, Glasgow. The date was May 10 1947 and the teams for that historic occasion were as follows:

GREAT BRITAIN : Swift (England), Hardwick (England) capt, Hughes (Wales), McCauley (Scotland), Vernon (Ireland), Burgess (Wales), Matthews (England), Mannion (England), Lawton (England), Steel (Scotland), Liddell (Scotland).

REST of EUROPE: Da Rui (France), Peterson (Denmark), Steffen (Switzerland), Carey (Eire) capt, Parola (Italy), Ludl (Czech.), Lambrechts (Belgium), Gren (Sweden), Nordahl (Sweden), Wilkes (Holland), Praest (Denmark).

Referee : George Reader.

Billed as The Match of the Century, the game was the brainchild of Stanley Rous, who proposed the fixture in order to celebrate the return of the home international countries to FIFA, and to raise much needed funds for the financially embarrassed world governing body.

When the game was officially announced to the public, discussion raged in the national press as to the possible line-up of the British team. Numerous competitions were conducted by the leading newspapers to correctly forecast the players who would represent Great Britain.

Those of us in contention for a place in the team were well aware of the competitions, and when the press finally revealed their poll results, many of the entrants were kind enough to choose me in their starting eleven.

The venue, Hampden Park, had one of the largest capacities of any ground in Europe at that time, so it was the ideal stadium to stage the match.

I was informed of my selection by Boro manager David Jack and that Wilf Mannion had also been chosen. In fact our double call-up was quite an accolade for Middlesbrough FC because they were the only club who had two representatives in the match. That was a remarkable achievement and one acknowledged by the local Evening Gazette which stated:

"They bring distinction to Middlesbrough FC... The selectors have paid a great tribute to the Borough, the only club to supply two players for the great test."

David Jack also had a further surprise to reveal from the contents of the official letter the club had received from the FA. It stated that George Hardwick had been chosen to captain the Great Britain side.

The honour I felt at being given the opportunity to lead "one hell of team" was immense. I was delighted. It was the ultimate accolade. What more could I personally achieve in the game? I was simultaneously the captain of Middlesbrough, England and Great Britain. What was left, possibly only to be elected Prime Minister!

The team assembled a few days before the game in Scotland at the Forest Hills Hotel, which nestled at the foot of the Trossachs, by the side of the tranquil Loch Ard, Aberfoyle, in Perthshire.

Ironically, even though it was one of the most prestigious and unique games in footballing history, Wilf and I made our own way to the team's headquarters by train, and then claimed our travelling expenses from the FA, whose attitude towards the reimbursement of money, I have previously mentioned, at best could be described as very frugal.

I recall filing one legitimate claim for a taxi fare which was returned part-paid with the reply that they felt the overall amount being claimed was rather excessive. So I ended up out of pocket in order to play for my country. The modern day professionals don't know how lucky they are!

When I arrived at the hotel and saw the calibre of player relaxing in the lounge I realised I was in exalted company. Great players of that era like Frank Swift, Billy Hughes, Archie McCauley, Jackie Vernon, Ronnie Burgess, Stan Matthews, Tommy Lawton, Wilf Mannion, Billy Steel and Billy Liddell, plus the reserves Raich Carter and George Young.

The powers that be had certainly chosen a well balanced side to represent the four home nations, with outstanding individuals in every position. It made you appreciate the strength in depth and the undoubted potential of a British side at that time, particularly when players of the quality of Tom Finney weren't even selected.

I firmly believe that if we'd entered a World Cup tournament with that team we would have returned triumphant, holding aloft the coveted gold Jules Rimet Trophy.

Aberfoyle was a quiet idyllic setting in which to practice with our manager Walter Winterbottom and his trainer Hughie Shaw. We were treated with great kindness and accorded celebrity status by the locals, many of whom came to watch us train on a local school playing field. The young children, in particular, followed us everywhere we went, politely asking for autographs.

Even though, to all intents and purposes, the fixture was an exhibition match we adopted a very professional approach towards the game. It was to be a showpiece occasion and we were determined to win and uphold the prestige of British football.

I wish I could have bottled and preserved the team spirit and camaraderie that existed between the players during that very special week. We had a marvellous time relaxing and training together. In an ideal world it should have lasted forever because we enjoyed each other's company so much. It was possibly the most splendid seven days in my footballing career.

In hindsight, if I was being totally honest with myself, and the match had been an ordinary league game, I most certainly would not have played because I wasn't fully fit. But because it was a once in a lifetime experience I just couldn't afford to miss out.

Prior to the match I believe the British side had a distinct advantage over the Europeans because, in common with England, most of us had played forces football together during the war and we knew our team-mates' strengths and weaknesses and could adapt our play accordingly.

The reaction of the predominantly Caledonian crowd at Hampden Park towards the English lads was strangely perverse, because it was the only time throughout my career that I've had the Scots shouting positive encouragement in my direction. Normally it was something to do with questioning the validity of my Sassenach parentage, even though I'm of Scottish descent. Normal service was resumed when England beat Scotland 2-0 the following April.

On the matchday we were allotted the home dressing-room and wore the dark blue shirts of Scotland which carried a square commemorative badge. There were over 134,000 people in the ground that afternoon, which at the time I believe was a European record.

Apparently interest in the fixture was so great that the ticket allocation could have been sold several times over, and the hundreds of foreign spectators and journalists present only served to give the game a truly international flavour.

When we walked out on to the pitch, flanked by bearers holding brightly coloured flags, the cacophony of sound which hit us was deafening.

Prior to the kick-off we were presented to Mr Jules Rimet, the President of FIFA, and Mr J Westwood, Secretary for Scotland.

The European team on that famous day was skippered by my great friend, Manchester United and Eire's fine half-back Johnny Carey, and contained some able Scandinavian forwards such as

Gren, Nordahl and Praest. In fact it was the latter who cut past me to set up their only goal.

Overall, the game was a contest for only about half an hour. It became a rather one-sided affair after we'd scored two early goals which knocked the stuffing out of the Continental opposition.

Great Britain went on to win rather comfortably 6-1, with Tommy Lawton and Wilf, both of whom put on superb individual performances, each scoring twice. A great solo effort by Morton's Billy Steel, and an own goal by the Italian centre-half Parola, completed the route.

After the match we attended the formal dinner at a Glasgow hotel with all the officials and dignitaries and I made a short speech thanking our opponents on behalf of the Great Britain team.

Some time later the players and reserves were presented with a small engraved unique shield to commemorate the only time a Great Britain team has played a competitive match.

We were also paid a nominal match fee, but the money was totally irrelevant because it was the prestige of the occasion which was important. If the truth be known I would have gladly paid them to be in the starting line-up on that special day.

We were permitted to keep the blue shirt as a memento, and even though Wilf and I were recognized and chatted happily to our fellow passengers, most of whom has attended the match, there were no reserved seats for us on the train journey home. We had to stand up most of the way back from Glasgow to Darlington. Again how times have changed. But in those days you just accepted the travelling inconveniences because it went with the job. We played football because we loved the game and not for any financial rewards. There were none.

What a marvellous and unique week in my footballing life, and one which I will treasure forever.

A week after the match against the Rest of the World I was back on England duty as a member of the sixteen strong squad which left RAF Northolt by Dakota for a tour of Switzerland and Portugal. Also selected were Wilf and the Middlesbrough's promising young full-back, Dicky Robinson. For the Boro to provide three players for an England squad was quite an achievement when I think of all the great players who were available during that era. If any of the big city clubs had supplied three players out of a continental touring party of sixteen it would have made back page headlines in the nationals.

Unfortunately the impressive statistic was only worth a passing mention, which leads me to note that I feel we in the North-east are often victims of our own self modesty. Over the years Middlesbrough has produced and developed some of this country's outstanding footballing talent, including Tim Williamson, George Elliott, Jacky Carr, Mick Fenton, George Camsell, George Hardwick, Wilf Mannion, Brian Clough, Alan Peacock, Mick McNeil, Willie Maddren, David Armstrong and Gary Pallister to name but a few.

What we need to do as an area is to be more positive and proud of our sporting heritage, and not only in football. It's about time a centre, specifically designated to acknowledge local sporting achievement, was given some serious consideration within the Teesside area.

Our base in Switzerland was the Dolder Grand Hotel situated in the picturesque mountains a few miles from the Grasshoppers of Zurich football ground, which was to be the venue for the match.

The facilities at the hotel were first class, including courts for badminton and a golf course, on which many of the players relaxed.

Stanley Matthews was, as I recall, the most accomplished golfer in the team and he seemed to spend most of his spare time out on the lush fairways with Dicky Robinson. In fact it was thanks to Robbo that I won a bet out on the course.

As it was his first tour, Dicky was something of an unknown quantity as a golfer. But I knew his shot making potential because I'd seen him play at Middlesbrough. So, when after a couple of holes, he managed to stymie himself behind two large trees, I had no hesitation in betting the lads that he would clear the timber and land the ball close to the flag.

In all honesty it was a very difficult shot to make, so the other players, including Tommy Lawton, Frank Swift and Stan Matthews, all quickly accepted my generous odds.

Dicky, I am pleased to say, did me proud. He made perfect contact with the ball and it sailed over the trees before landing softly in the heart of the green. It sometimes pays to have inside information. I cleaned up.

The idyllic training ground we were allocated was owned by the Swiss National Bank. Situated in a beautiful rural setting I remember we had to clear a wide variety of animal life from the pitch, including chickens and rabbits, before we could begin our practice sessions with Walter Winterbottom.

Those sessions were never over strenuous and comprised mainly of some gentle sprint work followed by ball skills, basic tactics and shooting practice at our goalkeeper, Frank Swift.

During my career I saw many players who were dedicated professionals but none more than Stanley Matthews. We often shared a room together and even in those days before players' dietary and vitamin intakes were fully studied by sports scientists, Stan had designed his own individual fitness regime. In fact Stan would often indulge in extra training on his own. It certainly paid dividends because his illustrious playing career continued at the top level for Blackpool and Stoke City until he was over fifty.

I would also like to correct a little inaccuracy which seems to have somehow slipped quietly into local football folklore. It's the one about George Hardwick finding Stanley Matthews so difficult to contain as an opponent that he often had a tactical injury when we faced Blackpool after the war.

The statistics I am glad to say prove otherwise. Out of eight possible matches against the Seasiders between 1946 and 1950 I played in six. And of those six Middlesbrough only lost one. So much for the myth that Hardwick didn't like facing Blackpool and Matthews.

In fact following one match at Ayresome Park, in October 1948, Stanley told the press, after our 1-0 victory, that I had been "in great form" and had stopped him from playing. The press reports of the time also confirmed Stan's synopsis:

"An interesting sideline was the duel between Matthews and Hardwick who are so often companions in the England teams. It was a refreshing, scrupulously clean conflict and Hardwick's success against his crafty rival helped considerably towards Middlesbrough's victory."

Without fear of contradiction I can honestly say I never shirked a challenge on the football field in my entire life and I've got some physical mementos to prove it.

When you are guests of another country they often do their utmost to to make your stay as pleasant as possible. And prior to the Swiss game our hosts arranged for the England team to have an "entertaining" night at the ballet.

The reaction of the lads when I told them we were being treated to an evening of culture is not printable. But in a situation like that you have no option but to accept the invitation, so we all reluctantly trooped off to the theatre to "enjoy" ourselves.

It was like taking a busload of kids to the pictures, because after about ten minutes most of the lads had come to end of their attention spans and began shuffling around in their seats.

Poor Walter Winterbottom could see there may be a problem so the message was hastily passed down the line to: "Please see it out till the interval." We acknowledged his request and sat patiently not wishing to insult our hosts.

As the curtain fell to conclude the first half we all quickly adjourned upstairs to the bar for a drink. As we entered the lounge there was a guy playing a piano in the corner and the convivial atmosphere was much more our liking.

Eventually, the great Blackpool forward, Stan Mortensen, asked if he could play the piano and proceeded to give us a rendition of the only tune he knew, Chopsticks, and even then you would have been hard pressed to recognise it through all the wrong notes.

As the bell went to announce the start of the second half we decided to stay put, and by the end of the night we were dancing our own ballet, the Hokey Cokey.

As for the empty seats, well apparently it was explained that we had decided to have an early night to conserve our energy for the big game. Very tactful.

Playing against England always created great interest abroad, and Zurich was no exception.

By kick-off time, the compact stadium was full to capacity with many of the keen fans, who were unable to get tickets, standing on the flat roofs surrounding the ground trying to gain a more suitable vantage point from which to watch the proceedings.

The game itself was a total disappointment from an English point of view. We lost 1-0. But to be fair there were mitigating circumstances.

The match was played on a very small pitch which gave us no opportunity to spread the ball wide to Stan Matthews. It was also the first time we had encountered the continental tactic of deploying a deep lying centre-forward. Until then, the number on your shirt designated where you played on the pitch, but not on that occasion. Their numbering system confused us, and I failed to spot it.

As captain it was my responsibility to quickly unravel the opposition tactics on the pitch. But early on in the game their formation caused us some real problems. Neil Franklin, our centre-half, found himself with nobody to mark and their little inside-right Willie Fink scored while we were coming to terms with their unique style of play.

Once I'd adjusted our own system, by detailing Eddie Lowe of Aston Villa to pick up the deep lying centre-forward, and had told Neil Franklin to stay back and cover the runs of their inside forwards, we began to cope with their formation and totally dominated the match.

It was, however, the kind of game you played in from time to time when no matter what you did, or how many chances you created, eventually you realised your team was never going to score. We hit the post and crossbar I don't know how many times, had shots cleared off the line, goals disallowed for offside and, as always happens in games of that nature, their goalkeeper played like a man inspired. I don't think we could have done any more than we did to win the game. On the day we just had no luck.

The English press, however, did not see it from my viewpoint. They were not at all sympathetic to our misfortune. In fact they crucified our performance, and we left for Geneva to play a Swiss B XI in practice match, with their negative comments ringing in our ears.

We did well to achieve a goalless draw in Geneva, having to perform on an atrociously uneven pitch. In addition, we fielded a team containing five changes so that we could give the other squad members some match practice. With the Swiss games completed, we flew to Lisbon in a four-engined Skymaster for a game against Portugal.

I was looking forward to the game because the inside information which we had received from neutral observers was that the Portuguese were potentially one of the best teams in Europe at that time. And, in view of our mediocre results in Switzerland, the game had taken on a much greater significance.

We were based for the match in the salubrious coastal resort of Estoril, with its grand houses, finely manicured gardens and famous casino, which of course we frequented. Most of us had never seen such sumptuous surroundings.

The day of the game was an extraordinary experience. The match was played in Lisbon's impressive new white marble, horse-shoe shaped, 70,000 capacity stadium. It was breathtaking. The green baize of a pitch was made from perfect English turf imported from Cumberland, and in my experience was only rivalled by Wembley in its quality.

The highly polished stone dressing rooms were the most modern and ostentatious I'd ever changed in. It was a fabulous place. Every player had his own individual locker and shower cubicle, which certainly was a vast improvement on the unhygienic, communal, muddy bathwater we all had to share in the depths of an English winter. Each of us had a personal bathrobe and a pair of sandals to wear while we were walking round the changing rooms. For some of the lads it was the height of decadence and they paraded up and down like Arab sheiks. The facilities resembled those you would expect to find in a five star hotel rather than a football ground, and it really put the standard of antiquated changing accommodation at English grounds to shame.

Before the match Neil Franklin passed a late fitness test, but because of a cut eye Blackburn Rovers' Bob Langton was replaced on the left wing by Tom Finney. That was some replacement, and again epitomised the terrific strength within the whole English squad at that time.

My team talk, prior to the match, was succinct and straight to the point. I simply said: "Right lads, let's shove the press criticism back down their throats." That's the polite way of putting it. In fact, I probably really told the players that the criticism should be shoved up some part of the pressmen's anatomy. Anyway, the team all agreed with the sentiments I'd expressed.

We emerged, in determined mood, from a marble tunnel into a stadium bathed in brilliant sunshine to be introduced to the President of Portugal.

After the pleasantries were complete, however, there was great controversy because a heated argument was soon raging about the size of the ball.

The Portuguese officials wanted to play with a size four, the type of ball used by the schoolboys back home. But Walter Winterbottom and myself felt that in many ways it would belittle the prestige of the international fixture and we both insisted on a full size five.

The Continental referee, as I recall, spoke very little English, which did little to help the situation. I had great difficulty, much to the amusement of the rest of the lads, making myself understood. Eventually, after much gesticulating, we convinced him to begin with the regulation ball.

The furore over the ball only served to make the lads more resolute, because within thirteen seconds of the kick-off Tommy Lawton had headed us in front. From then on we systematically dismantled the opposition.

After the opening goal their keeper deliberately switched the ball, which was a little bit naughty under the circumstances. No doubt he was following instructions, but we ended up with the size four ball which we didn't want. However we were so outstanding that day that the size of the ball was immaterial. The speed of our passing, the movement into space, the individual skill and the clinical finishing were at times bewildering. In fact we could have played with a tennis ball and still won.

We led 5-0 by half-time, and as the goals tally steadily mounted, so the anger of the jeering crowd became more intense. Their derision was primarily directed towards the unfortunate goalkeeper Azevedo, who eventually became so frustrated at constantly retrieving the ball from the back of the net that he removed his jersey and threw it in the direction of the reserve keeper, before walking off the pitch in disgust. In those days there was no formal system of substitution in operation but the referee just shrugged his shoulders and allowed them to change.

The changeover made little difference to the progress of the match as Tom Finney in particular repeatedly cut the Portuguese defence to ribbons.

Despite the searing 90 degrees heat, which we certainly were not used to back home in England, we continued with our majestic display in the second half. All our rampant forwards, with the exception of Wilf, scored that day, and when the final whistle blew, we had thrashed the Portuguese team 10-0.

In fact their humiliated players were so ashamed and embarrassed by the result that they failed to attend the formal evening banquet. It was a decision for which they were later suspended by their FA. At the time, however, we didn't mind because the early finish to the formal proceedings gave us more time to sample the delights of the Portuguese nightlife. I'm glad to report that we found it very much to our liking.

That match in Lisbon was possibly the most complete attacking team performance I ever played in. It should not be assumed that because we won by such a large score, that it was due to the opposition being sub-standard. The forward line, which had borne the brunt of the barbed newspaper criticism for our dismal displays in Zurich and Geneva, was in marvellous form with Stan Mortenson and Tommy Lawton both scoring four times and Stan Matthews and Tom Finney completing the route.

It was a pleasant sojourn in the sun which boosted our confidence to face Belgium in Brussels at the start of the new season.

At the beginning of the new international campaign, in September 1947, we continued where we'd left off in Lisbon the previous season. We were in a very confident mood for the match against the Belgians at the Hysel Stadium.

That encounter turned out to be a *tour de force* for Stan Matthews, who played one of the international matches of his life.

The tone for the match was set as early as the opening minute when The Wizard of the Dribble mesmerized the Belgian defence with one of his trademark jinking runs and provided Tommy Lawton with the opportunity to score.

From then on there was no holding Stan, who had an inspired game, creating a host of chances from which Tom Finney and Stan Mortensen consolidated our superiority against a very game, but totally outclassed, home team. We were always in control and cruised to a 5-2 victory.

After our convincing victory in Brussels, we came to Cardiff to tackle Wales in October full of confidence.

As usual, the passionate Welsh vocal support created a fervent atmosphere inside the ground, but my experienced England team had developed the ability over the previous matches to strike quickly and subdue the home fans' ardour.

The beginning of the match was almost a carbon copy of the opening period in Lisbon and Brussels, because within fifteen minutes we were leading 3-0, thanks to goals by scored by Tom Finney, Stan Mortensen and Tommy Lawton. The game was effectively over as a contest.

Although, to their credit, the Welsh lads staged a second half rally, defensively we played well with Swifty and Neil Franklin in particularly outstanding form.

Wales at Ninian Park were usually a very tough proposition indeed, as they were able to call on the skills of quality players like Wally Barnes and Bryn Jones. In fact at one time in the 1930s, Jones had been the most expensive player in the country when he was transferred to Arsenal. On the day, the standard of our forward play was excellent, prompting one newspaper reporter to remark after the match:

"England's soccer is experiencing one of its finest hours."

I wouldn't argue with that verdict because England at the time had a very settled team, with fine players who knew their specific roles. Also, and very importantly, I must repeat that team morale off the field was high. We were an outstanding side, or so we thought.

If ever a game brought a team back down to earth it was the explosive fixture played, in November 1947, against Northern Ireland in front of a nearly 68,000 people at a packed Goodison Park, in Liverpool.

We had won our three previous international games very convincingly, scoring no fewer than eighteen goals in the process.

As a result we were receiving many plaudits, quite rightly in my opinion, from the national press about the high quality and standard of our all round play.

But we began to believe our own publicity after reading headlines claiming that Irish would be: *"Next for the English chopping block."*

As a team we failed to remember a couple of old football adages which state: 1, Never underestimate the strength of the opposition; and 2, Avoid becoming complacent.

For 75% of the game we were totally outfought by an Irish side containing two Evertonians, Eglington and Farrell, who played their hearts out on their home ground. In addition there was the admirable Peter Doherty, whose probing solo runs constantly put our defence under pressure.

The Irish lads played with great spirit and determination throughout, and deservedly took the lead just after the interval with a goal from Walsh.

I thought it was definitely not going to be our day when we were awarded a rather dubious penalty after Jackie Vernon had allegedly fouled Stan Matthews, and Wilf proceeded to have the spot kick brilliantly saved by Hinton. The contentious decision had led to prolonged protests by all the Irish players but justice was probably served when we failed to take the opportunity.

To our credit we used Wilf's miss as a springboard to set up a grandstand finish, with three goals being scored in the last few minutes. Firstly we equalised when Wilf scored from a pass by Billy Wright, and before the cheering had died down Tommy Lawton converted a cross from Stan Matthews to put us in front.

We appeared to be heading for a very unlikely victory, when in the final minute, the unpredictable Doherty played a sharp one-two on the edge of our box and slipped his shot past Frank Swift into the net for a 2-2 draw which, in all honesty, the Irish lads' progressive play had fully deserved.

Although the game had ended in a rousing finish it could not hide the fact that we had been given the runaround and were outfought for most of the afternoon. It provided even the most seasoned English professional with a salutary reminder that you should at all times have the utmost respect for the opposition.

A fortnight after our disappointing draw against Northern Ireland, we played host to Sweden's first full international match on a miserable damp November afternoon in front of a crowd of 50,000 at Highbury.

The Swedes were a very competent side and their fine centre-forward Gunnar Nordahl had played for the Rest of Europe against Great Britain at Hampden Park.

By half-time we had established a comfortable 3-1 lead thanks to a couple of goals from Stan Mortensen and a penalty by Tommy Lawton. I was, however, to have a very eventful second period which started with me striking the crossbar with a powerful free kick. Then, with Swifty beaten, I cleared a shot off the line as the Swedes pressed forward trying to get back into the game.

As the half continued I momentarily collapsed after blocking a goalbound shot with my head. Again another example of where there's no sense there's no feeling. And obviously I'd remembered little of my experience at Stoke City in 1938.

My exploits were completed when I was adjudged to have fouled Gunnar Nordahl in the area for a Swedish penalty which they converted to reduce the deficit to 3-2. Those Swedish lads made us fight every inch of the way.

Morty, however, saved me any further embarrassment when he completed his hat-trick on the stroke of full time to give us a deserved 4-2 victory over determined and worthy opponents.

It was a match where I never seemed to far away from the centre of the action. But there again I wouldn't have had it any other way.

I was once again a very proud man as I led England out on April 10, 1948, into that hostile Hampden Park atmosphere. This was another Scotland v England battle, so it was no surprise that the wall of sound which greeted me it was the total antithesis of the warm reception I'd received as the captain of Great Britain the previous year. There was something very special about playing the Scots at Hampden Park and I was looking forward to the game. But little did I know that it was to be my final international match, both as an England player, and captain of my country.

Right from the outset the Scots seemed hell-bent on stopping us playing our normal passing game. Instead of the match being a football showpiece, it was more like a confrontational showdown with destructive tactics being employed by our opponents.

Despite their deliberate intent, Tom Finney managed to score a fine individual goal to give us the lead before half-time.

In the second period, as the ferocity of the physical contact took its toll, our goalkeeper Frank Swift was smashed to the ground by Liverpool forward Billy Liddell and played the rest of the game with broken ribs. Normally I would have taken over in goal as emergency cover, allowing Frank to leave the field for treatment, but I spent the final few minutes of the second half hobbling around out on the wing with my left knee strapped, after an accidental collision with the Scots' right winger Jimmy Delaney.

For most of the game his only move had been to try and jink outside me down the touchline, but by closing down the space I'd managed to keep him quiet. Then, in the second half, after making an interception, I turned inside on my left foot, bringing the ball with me. At the same time Delaney's momentum caused him to plough into my back and the full force of his body crashed down on my left knee. I felt a sharp snap and then a strange sensation as if the leg was floating in the breeze. In those days, you only came off the field if you could not stand up, especially as there were no substitutes. So, when some feeling returned to my leg, I decided to grin and bear it. I managed to keep going thanks to the strapping, and hobbled through to the final whistle.

Later, an examination established that I'd torn the lateral ligament in my left knee, which prematurely finished my season.

We were determined not to be intimidated by the Scots and sealed a hard fought victory when Stan Mortensen scored our second to finally dampen the over zealous enthusiasm of both the Scottish crowd and their team.

The match was the most physical of encounters and typical of fixtures between the Auld Enemy. Reports at the time referred to the game being punctuated by:

"A long and sickening succession of fouls, free kicks and stoppages for injuries."

As my last international match it was certainly one to remember and I'm sure I still have the bruises to prove it.

Due to my injury I was not chosen the following month for Frank Swift's finest international display in England's marvellous 4-0 win against Italy in Turin.

What I didn't realise at the time was when I informed Sir Stanley Rous that I would be unable to captain the FA summer tour to the Continent, I was in fact phoning the death knell on my international career.

And even though I regained my fitness and played well for Middlesbrough during the 1948/49 season, I was never chosen to play for my country again, despite having my ardent supporters in the national press:

"Middlesbrough's skipper George Hardwick has played some outstanding football this season, equally as good as when he was an automatic choice for his country. If he is overlooked on this form, then there would appear to be little hope of his playing again for England. Hardly fair treatment for a man who has been one of England's greatest football ambassadors.

"Hardwick, the best captain I have seen this season, is still a master tactician and a full-back who always tries to use the ball. Watch how many of Boro's attacks begin with a neatly-placed clearance from Gentleman George."

I thought I could have played at least two more years at international level but at the time there seemed to be some unwritten policy that if an England captain lost his place in the side it was almost impossible for him to return. Perhaps it might not have been the end of my international career if I had not been the captain. That is something which I will never know.

I had gained so much pleasure from being an England international. I was immensely proud to lead my country into battle against the cream of Europe's footballers. But, however well I played for Middlesbrough, there was no way back. Whenever the international line-up was named, my name was always missing. Outwardly I endeavoured to remain philosophical about my exclusion but inside I was deeply disappointed to have lost the captaincy of my country.

• SEVEN •

Hardwick's International Hall of Fame

Football is a game of wide-ranging personal opinion and a reflection of people's individual preferences. The inept tactical decisions made by the manager, and who should be playing in which position, have always been subjects for heated debate in the pubs and clubs, no matter in which era you watched your football. That's what makes the game so intriguing.

The great misconception amongst the supporters of today when we discuss the players from my generation is that they would have been ineffective in the modern game. I disagree entirely.

Ability and talent evolve with the changes in the game. Granted, the contemporary game is much faster and the training techniques vastly different, but the players of my era could only have benefitted greatly from a stable political situation, the advances in the medical treatment, the lightweight kit, and the wider understanding of dietary needs. So I feel the comparative argument is flawed.

What we must enjoy is the talent that every new generation of players possesses, because unless you take into account the time, place and circumstances, comparisons are meaningless.

I have often been asked who, in my opinion, was the most influential player of my era. It is an almost impossible question to answer because so many of the players of that period had outstanding, yet differing attributes. For example:

STAN MATTHEWS (Stoke City & Blackpool) was nicknamed The Wizard of the Dribble. A right winger with quick feet and a change of pace which could mesmerize the opposition and alter the course of a match in a split second. Stan's main attribute was his confidence on the ball and the self belief that he would always beat the full-back and create chances for other members of the team. A career spanning four decades is testimony to his unique ability.

TOMMY LAWTON (Everton & Chelsea) was quite simply the best header of a ball I've ever seen. He had the ability to hang in the air above defenders before using his strong neck muscles to power the ball towards goal. A man with a great sense of humour, he was a tough and fearless centre-forward with a keen eye for goal who packed a lethal shot in either foot. Often great goalscorers are accused of being selfish but if Tommy saw a colleague in a better position he would always pass to capitalise on the opportunity.

FRANK SWIFT (Manchester City) was a tall, athletic and surprisingly agile goalkeeper for his size. He had total command of his penalty area and displayed great positional sense. He often acted as England's sweeper before the term had ever been coined. Swifty was also one of the first keepers to think about retaining possession of the ball by passing it out, basketball style, to our defenders rather than continually resorting to the aimless punt up field. He had hands the size of dinner plates and could easily pick up the ball one-handed. A man with a great sense of fun he was a real tonic on the training ground or in the dressing-room. How sad his life was ended prematurely in the Munich Air Disaster.

RAICH CARTER (Sunderland & Derby County) was an inside-forward who had a tremendous shot in both feet. Very tough, with a high degree of self-confidence which at times bordered on arrogance, he never wasted a pass and developed an excellent understanding with Stan Matthews down England's right flank.

WILF MANNION (Middlesbrough) played his football instinctively and had the ability, with one piece of individual magic, to turn a game in your favour. His great attributes were his exquisite first touch, balance, natural talent and an acute eye for openings which enabled him to score goals as well as create them.

NOEL FRANKLIN (Stoke City) was the best centre-half I played with. No arguments. He had an uncanny ability to read the game and snuff out danger. Like all great footballers he seemed to have time in which to play and his calm, perceptive distribution of the ball often began a decisive counterattack. What a pity he virtually ruined his international career by moving to Colombia against the advice of the FA.

LAURIE SCOTT (Arsenal) was my full-back partner on every occasion I played a full international for England. He was quick, good in the tackle and along with Frank Swift we formed a solid defensive triangle for nearly two international seasons after the war.

PETER DOHERTY (Manchester City) was always an awkward opponent because he was unpredictable and at times appeared to be totally unco-ordinated. He was a defender's nightmare. As he ran, there always seemed to be a great flurry of arms and legs and a ball which appeared out of control. The flame-haired Irishman may have looked unorthodox but he was a gifted dribbler who combined a high work rate with precision passing and ability to score in the tightest of situations.

STAN MORTENSEN (Blackpool) Although rather frail looking, Morty was one of the toughest and most dynamic players of my era. Quick off the mark, he bravely recovered from the injuries he'd sustained in a plane crash to become one of the most lethal goalscoring international forwards of his generation. His record of nearly a goal a game for England speaks for itself.

JOHNNY CAREY (Manchester United) was a truly versatile and highly respected international footballer. Captain of Eire, he was a man with an unflappable reputation whose shrewd passing ability and incisive tackling was equally as effective at either wing-half or inside-forward. A great friend, he was deservedly voted player of the year in 1948/49.

But if I had to chose one player from my playing days who exhibited everything in terms of talent, and importantly temperament, then I would cast my vote for The Preston Plumber.

TOM FINNEY (Preston N.E.) not only possessed great natural ability in both feet, but he was an adaptable player, very versatile, and scored goals consistently throughout his distinguished career. He had a deceptive change of pace which left defenders floundering, and was just as effective at inside-forward, centre-forward or out on the wing. Coupled with his natural talent Tom is a real gentleman and thoroughly deserved his knighthood for services to football.

· EIGHT ·

Crossing the boundary line

There were many weeks of protracted negotiations and arguments over whether I had the right to a free transfer at Ayresome Park. It was certainly very clear that I could not play on for very much longer in the First Division because of the problems with my knee. One way or the other, I would not be playing for the Boro in the near future.

However, a contract was for life as far as a football club was concerned in those days, and the club held all the aces in our negotiations. So it was not surprising that the matter dragged on for some time. In the end the tug-of-war was sorted out when Oldham Athletic finally agreed to pay Middlesbrough a fee of £15,000 to acquire my services. It was a large fee in those days, especially for a Third Division club.

As I have said before, I loved Middlesbrough Football Club. But I knew that a new chapter in my life was ready to begin and I was very much looking forward to taking control of the Oldham team, using my coaching experience and putting my ideas into practice.

Once Boro had accepted Oldham's offer, I officially signed for The Latics following a meeting held between the representatives of both clubs at Ayresome Park on November 7, 1950. The huge fee was put into perspective by the fact that at the time it was the highest amount ever paid for a full-back.

When I left Middlesbrough, contrary to scurrilous speculation in certain quarters, the club and myself parted on the best of terms. There was no ill-feeling on either side, and the parting of the ways was both mutual and cordial. In fact the manager, David

Jack wrote some very kind remarks in his match programme notes following my departure, for which I was very grateful:

"George Hardwick has the satisfaction of knowing that his last game for the Borough was a classic as far as he was personally concerned. I cannot remember him putting a foot wrong. He is leaving the top flight two or three years too soon but sees the Oldham player/manager's job as a great opportunity and everybody on Teesside will wish a grand footballer the very best of luck in his new venture."

Nearly fifty years ago Oldham Athletic were a club in the lower reaches of the Third Division North, suffering from stagnation and deep inertia. Despite my strong belief in my ability as a coach, I knew that I faced an enormous task to resurrect the club's fortunes. However the only way for their fortunes to move was up. And on my arrival at the ground I even boldly declared in the local press: *"Promotion in two years is my ambition."*

I was appointed player/manager at a time when fulfiling that dual role was quite a new innovation. The out-dated FA regulations, however, failed to keep up with the pace of change and stipulated that, despite my extra responsibility and workload, I could still only receive a player's wage. So I certainly didn't make the move across the Pennines for the money.

But I did need control of all team affairs if I was to make the right impact at Boundary Park. Right from the outset of my appointment I cultivated a fine working relationship with the chairman, Stanley Cheetham, and it was he more than anybody who gave me the decision-making independence I desired.

I quickly immersed myself in every aspect of the day to day running of the club, adopting the principle of, if you want a job doing, do it yourself.

Eventually my role evolved into being a player, trainer, coach, manager and assistant groundsman. All for the princely sum of £8 a week plus bonuses.

Although I formally began my duties as player/manager of Oldham in the autumn it wasn't until the following April that my family and I moved permanently to the Oldham area. The delay was necessary because Joy had just had our second child, Andrew, and it would have been difficult to leave our home in Saltburn while he was so young.

The winter of 1950/51 was a very difficult period for me. I was travelling across the Pennines on average three times a week through a wide variety of climatic conditions often akin to those experienced by participants in the Monte Carlo Rally. This was long before the M62 was constructed, and so the journey was a lot more difficult than it is in the present day. It was also a lot slower, especially when there was snow and ice on the top of the hills.

Despite the inclement weather conditions, however, I never once failed to make that journey from Teesside. I enjoyed every second of my new role with Oldham and I think that my determination to get to my desk, despite the worst which the British climate could throw at me, emphasised my commitment to my new job.

The upheaval of moving to a new club can be unsettling and it is an aspect of a professional footballer's life which is not often fully appreciated by the majority of supporters. Depending on the individual, it can take quite a while to adjust to a new environment and sort out your domestic arrangements. Most professional players, from whatever era, will tell you that if you are experiencing personal problems off the field, then your performance on it is bound to suffer. However, I was determined to give the job my best, and also to lead the players by example.

When I arrived at Boundary Park there was a depressing mood of apathy in the dressing-room. Many of the players on the books had been in league football for some time and did not have a lot to offer. They were coming to the end of their careers and had no desire to improve themselves or Oldham Athletic. There was an air of a club resigned to constant mediocrity.

Out on the pitch the team's general performance and attitude was poor, and they played with no real tactical plan or formation. My primary objective, therefore, was to teach them, and I use the word teach deliberately, how I wanted the game played. I was determined to stamp my personality on the team and get the best out of the available players. Even at that advanced stage of their careers, I knew I could make them better players and hopefully give them a renewed zest for the game.

After a hard struggle, during which time 21,000 people came to see my debut against Lincoln City, we managed to finish the league season in a 15th position. I thought it was respectable considering the managerial upheaval and I saw it as a positive step in the right direction.

In my first few months in charge I played in three different positions, and covered almost every blade of the pitch at times. In fact I discovered another string to my bow by scoring seven goals in 21 appearances. It was my most prolific season ever.

Even after only half a season in the job I was convinced that I could build an attractive side at Oldham. In fact, because of Boundary Park's large capacity and pulling power, I quickly realised that the crowd potential was enormous.

Ironically, I had no sooner moved from the North-east than I was back again, staying at a hotel in my home town of Saltburn and training on the beach with my new club. That was because we had been drawn to play Hartlepools United in the second round of the FA Cup at the Victoria Ground in the December.

Hartlepools were in the same division at the time, but the Cup tie seemed to give the match an added edge. My return to the North-east grabbed the imagination of the Hartlepools public and there was a great atmosphere before the kick-off. Detailed local coverage of my swift return to familiar surroundings helped to swell the crowd to a near 15,000 capacity.

I knew that Hartlepools would try to set about us from the start and I was right. My new charges were given a torrid time in the first half by the home forwards, who scored a deserved early goal. From then on our penalty area was like the Alamo. We were being bombarded from all areas and we struggled to cope.

It stayed that way until mid-way through the second period when, fortuitously for us, and totally against the run of play, Hartlepools conceded an own goal. That incident changed the whole pattern of the game completely. Billy Ormond scored our second and decisive goal soon afterwards, and we then managed to hang on to our lead. We came through it together as a team, which was very important to me and I was proud of my players afterwards. I felt that I had led by example, with the local press kindly noting that:

"Hardwick was holding the defence together with his cool generalship."

It was a victory which, in the early stages of the game, had seemed most unlikely. But it turned out to be a very important success.

In the next round we were drawn away to Manchester United. It was a big day for my players, especially as United were on Oldham's doorstep and were revered as the nearest big club, along with Manchester City. Looking forward to the match helped keep my players on their toes, with everybody battling hard so that they could earn a place in the side to face United. Although we eventually lost 4-1, there were periods in the game when my old friend Matt Busby was certainly unnerved by the quality and determination of our play. We went down fighting and earned many new fans that day. That inspired performance gave the players a great confidence boost and before the end of the season we had recorded eleven league victories, which gave me a solid base from which to plan the new campaign.

Naturally a lot of my friends back home, and the Boro supporters, were taking a deep interest in my progress. Week after week during the early part of career at Oldham many people from Teesside sent me kind letters of support.

On one particular memorable occasion, when I was in hospital recovering from a knee operation, hundreds of get well cards crossed the Pennines and helped to cheer me up no end. It was a sign of the strong affinity between myself and the Teesside fans and I always have had a special place in my heart for them.

The Middlesbrough footballing public were also kept in constant touch with my progress in the manager's chair because I had weekly conversations with my good friend, Cliff Mitchell, the Evening Gazette's sports writer. Cliff used any interesting snippets of information which I could give him in his daily columns. He also kept me up to speed with happenings at Ayresome Park. It was very satisfying to know that I was not a forgotten man in my home town area.

During the summer break I was determined not to waste any valuable time. So I enrolled some willing members from the supporters club at Oldham to repair and repaint the stadium and dressing-rooms. This was a vital job because it appeared they had not been touched for years, and I wanted to improve and spruce up the working environment for my players. From the local traders I also scrounged the paint, cement and timber to tackle the much needed renovation.

Prior to the start of the 1951/52 season the club had little finance available with which to recruit fresh talent. So I began to raise the profile of Oldham by fostering links with the local community. It was a concerted effort to stop the haemorrhaging of local talent to the two flourishing Manchester clubs. There were many good young players in the North-west and it was important that Oldham brought their fair share of them to Boundary Park.

Night after night I held trial games at a nearby Lancashire League ground. By the end of those sessions I had enough good youngsters to field both junior and second team sides for the forthcoming season. It was a huge step in the right direction.

Also during that summer I was instrumental, along with Stanley Morgan, the local school's Physical Training Adviser, in establishing the first football coaching courses in the Oldham area. We were able to arrange these in conjunction with the Local Education Committee.

However, the availability of suitable outdoor training facilities was problematic because the local cinder pitches were hardly ideal surfaces on which to teach tackling skills. So the initial coaching sessions took place indoors at the Hollins Secondary School, in Lyndhurst Road. I was delighted that Jack Warner, the new wing-half I'd signed from Manchester United, was keen to come along to provide me with able assistance. The courses proved to be highly successful and were prominently featured in the local press.

As finance was at a premium, I made no apologies for utilising the old boys network which I'd established during my international playing career. It included contacting Matt Busby, manager of Manchester United, and David Jack of Middlesbrough, to see if they could release any experienced players, at suitably knock down prices, to give my new club that much needed fresh impetus.

Eventually, after many long hours spent bargaining in person and on the telephone, I managed to sign several young amateurs as well as four experienced players. They included Jack Warner from Manchester Utd, Pat Broadly from Sligo, Boro's Peter McKennan and Dennis Grainger from Wrexham.

McKennan, and his wonderful short-fuse of a Scottish temper, I knew well from my days with Chelsea and Middlesbrough. He had shattered his knee cap the previous season at Boro, but he was keen to continue playing and I knew that he could do a great job for Oldham. What a productive partnership he formed with Jack Warner. However, it was only productive on the field of play. Unfortunately, off the pitch, they rarely saw eye to eye and I was constantly having to act as referee and peacemaker when they were on another collision course. I reckon they shook hands more times to apologise to each other than I did with the opposition skippers.

My next radical innovation was to deliberately curtail the length of the close season to only three weeks. It was almost unheard of in those days, and the players were a little taken aback. They had been used to a much longer break. However, I believed that it would make a big difference to have all the players report back early for training. That strategy enabled me to devise concentrated sessions for fitness and tactics, instigate a fully structured coaching programme, and also assess each player's personal professional commitment to the club. I received an excellent response from the players and the shortened break was a major contributory factor towards us getting off to a great start the following season.

I can't discuss training at Oldham without mentioning one of the most loyal and hardworking sidekicks a manager could wish to have, namely Bill Thomas. Bill was a real character, a rough diamond, a man who spoke his mind, and I admired him for it. You knew where you stood with him, and the initial success I achieved at Boundary Park was partly due to Bill's enthusiasm and dedication.

I also noted quite early into my time at Oldham that the club had no formal badge, so psychologically the players had nothing to play for.

To create a successful football team I believe you need to have pride in your personal performance and a passionate commitment to the club for which you are playing. Designing a new shirt motif, fulfilled those objectives. I wanted the players to think positively about the club and about their job, and feel a sense of pride in wearing a distinctive badge.

Our pre-season hard work paid immediate dividends when we made a flying start to the new campaign. In fact we completed our first nine league games unbeaten, before it came to an end rather abruptly when we lost heavily by 5-2 at Bradford City. It was a significant defeat about which I will expand later.

Injuries to key players, however, myself included, meant that we couldn't sustain our challenge at the top of the division. We just didn't have a big enough squad of experienced players. For a long time there was a chance that we might come back into the promotion reckoning if we could put together a run of wins, but eventually we had to settle for a creditable fourth place. At the same time there was every reason to be satisfied by our overall efforts. We had proved ourselves an attractive and enterprising side by scoring a highly impressive 90 goals in the process.

Overall, I was very pleased with our position after my first full season in charge because I felt, both as a team and as a club, that we were definitely progressing in the right direction.

I was also pleased to see that we appeared to have captured the dormant interest of the local Oldham public. The average attendance for the season was 16,000, which no doubt pleased the directors, and served to confirm my initial observation about the club's crowd potential.

On the pitch I have two lasting memories of my first full season in charge at Boundary Park. The first was an outstanding individual performance from Eric Gemmell, who set a club goalscoring record by hitting the target seven times in our 11-2 thrashing of Chester on a freezing snow covered afternoon in January.

The second was rather different. It was suffering the personal indignity of being sent from the field of play for the one and only time in my career.

Strangely enough, in the first half of the Chester game, we fell behind 2-1 due to a couple of unfortunate mistakes made by our 16 year old goalkeeper. He had made his debut only the previous week because both of our regular choices between the sticks, Fred

Ogden and George Burnett, were injured. Little did we know, not only how the fortune of the team would change that day, but also that the young custodian called Eddie Hopkinson would later be capped by England, in a long and distinguished career with Bolton Wanderers.

To this day I feel the decision to send me off was totally unjustified. It created an unwanted indelible stain on my playing record. These days players can be sent off on several occasions during their careers and think nothing of it. But I always prided myself on fair play at a time when dismissals in football were few and far between. I would never have deliberately fouled an opponent in a manner which might have led to an early bath. Nor would I have resorted to throwing wild punches. Throughout my career I'd always thought of myself as a player who was hard but fair, and exhibited self-control and discipline on the pitch.

At Valley Parade, Bradford, however, following a harsh penalty award against us, there a mass brawl in the centre circle. As I attempted to separate the scuffling players I became embroiled in the unsavoury fracas.

During the prolonged and undignified melee, which did neither side any credit, I was deliberately kicked by the Bradford trainer Shufflebottom, who had initially come on to the pitch to attend to an injured player. What right Shufflebottom had to kick anybody, I don't know.

My instant reaction to his premeditated act was to push him away with my hands and remonstrate with the referee about the assault.

To my complete surprise, the referee, Mr Black, - I'll always remember his appropriate name - raised his right hand in the air, and gestured me towards the direction of the dressing-rooms. He'd sent me off.

As I walked in utter disbelief from the pitch, the highly antagonised and over emotional home crowd of 20,000 were baying for blood, mostly mine. The atmosphere became so hostile that one angry spectator athletically jumped the perimeter fencing and ran towards me before attempting to strike me. Fortunately he was subdued by a couple of officers from the local constabulary.

As I finally approached the relative safety of the dressing-rooms, a variety of missiles were thrown in my direction. In fact I received a direct hit on the back from a half-eaten apple.

I was so incensed and annoyed by what I considered to be a completely unjust decision that I demanded a personal hearing at FA headquarters about the incident.

I felt certain that my side of the unsavoury events would be accepted, and that I would be vindicated of the charge. I expected the sending off to be struck from the records. My protestations, however, were all to no avail. The footballing authorities upheld the dismissal, much to my disbelief, and I was eventually charged with misconduct and suspended for a fortnight.

During the whole of the proceedings, the referee remained adamant that he'd sent me off for deliberately striking an opponent, which simply wasn't true.

As a result of his intransigence my previously unblemished reputation disappeared overnight. What a pity that this was long before the days of television cameras, because if the incident had been captured on film then I would have had valuable video evidence with which to prove my case. However, at that time, all that the authorities had was my word against the word of Mr Black. And it was Mr Black who had the ear of the authorities.

Not long after I'd arrived at Oldham I formed an association of more mature players to carry on the charity work I'd started on Teesside. These players included some of my old friends, like Frank Swift. We strolled around the country to star in a series of benefit matches. We eventually developed links with various Showbiz XI's and travelled as far afield as Eire to raise funds for good causes. These games were personally very important because over the years many people had ensured that I achieved my ambition in life and I wanted to repay that encouragement by helping to raise money for both national and local charity organisations.

I vividly remember in one particular game in the 1960s at South Bank's ground in Middlesbrough when the Showbiz team included Tommy Steele, Harry Fowler, Andrew Ray, Ronnie Carroll, Billy Wright and Wally Barnes. They were playing my team of All-Stars. Unfortunately I left poor David Frost with a broken wrist after a tackle, though it was a complete accident.

Over the years many players and celebrities, too numerous to mention, have forgone their valuable free time to attend the many functions with which I have been involved. I would like to take this opportunity to thank them all for their support.

At the beginning of the 1952/53 season I managed to sign Tommy Lowrie from Aberdeen and the introduction of his ball winning and passing skills made me quietly confident I had assembled a team capable of winning promotion. There were a lot of capable players in the team by that time and they all wanted to do well for themselves and for the club.

My confidence was not unfounded. We lost only one of our first eighteen matches and topped the table. We played a lot of attractive football and rarely came up against a side which I felt was as good as us. In fact, right throughout the campaign I believed that we could win the title by a record number of points. Unfortunately, after the New Year we again suffered a spate of serious injuries which, because of our small squad, threatened our promotion prospects.

First, Nobby Clarke, who I had secured to fill the centre-forward berth, damaged a knee and had to enter hospital for an operation. Then shortly afterwards I joined him.

Curiously, my injury occurred in the club car park which we were using as a makeshift training pitch when all our other facilities were unavailable because of a heavy snowfall.

About half an hour into the session I attempted to turn sharply, but my foot remained firmly stuck in the snow, causing my left knee to twist and damage the cartilage. The injury was serious enough to require surgery at Ashton Hospital.

Those days in hospital were very frustrating, and although the kind people of Oldham sent me enough get well cards, flowers, fruit and sherry to supply all the other patients, the team in my absence lacked direction. As a result they lost five times in seven matches. I knew that if we were to secure promotion it was vital that I recovered quickly to raise the morale of both the players and supporters.

In normal circumstances, before the advent of modern keyhole surgery, recovering from a cartilage operation took months. But with just one reserve game under my belt I was back in first team action in time for the crucial final game of the season.

By that time Port Vale, managed by one of my old pals Freddie Steele, had mounted a strong challenge for the one available promotion place. It left us needing at least a point from our last match at Bradford City to deny them the championship.

Ironically Valley Parade was the very ground where I'd been dismissed the previous season. So you can imagine the warm "welcome" I received from the home support. It was not the ground that I would have deliberately selected in which to go back and try to secure promotion.

I will, however, always be grateful for the huge contingent of loyal Latics fans who crossed the Pennines that afternoon on April 29, 1953. We needed their tremendous backing from the terraces because, in all fairness, we didn't play well.

We were constantly under pressure and I remember having to make a couple of desperate goal-line clearances to keep us afloat. We did not create a great deal at the other end of the pitch. It was essentially a backs to the wall effort. But in the end the standard of performance was irrelevant, because we gained the precious point we required in a 0-0 draw.

The emotional scenes at the final whistle on that marvellous day, as I was chaired from the Valley Parade pitch, high on the shoulders of the ecstatic blue and white supporters, will live long in the memory. Oldham Athletic had won their first Championship in 46 years of league football and were promoted to Division Two.

Our achievement prompted jubilant celebrations throughout the Oldham area, and was a just reward for the consistent level of support the townspeople had given us during the course of the season. The average crowd had risen again, to over 17,000.

In appreciation of our achievement we were accorded a civic reception by the mayor, Councillor HB Whittaker, and I was officially thanked for putting the town firmly back on the football map. It was all very gratifying, but it was a team effort and I stressed that point absolutely clearly. I could not thank the players enough for their dedication and commitment during the season.

To round off the promotion party I took the players to the 1953 Cup Final at Wembley between Bolton and Blackpool. The match was to become known as The Matthews Final, and it turned out to be a classic. It was terrific to see my own mate Stan turn on the style on the biggest stage of them all. It was also a fine way to complete what had been a very successful season for both Oldham Athletic FC and their player/manager George Hardwick.

I received many letters of congratulation from Teesside and local sports writer Cliff Mitchell kindly wrote in his column:

"There is not the slightest doubt that Borough's old skipper is doing a grand job in his managerial capacity."

During the course of that year many of the leading national newspapers sent reporters to Boundary Park. There was, no doubt, a certain curiosity value in running the rule over how a former England captain was adjusting to life as a player/manager in the lower reaches of the Football League. Most of the articles, I am happy to say, were very positive and this report was typical of the attention I was receiving:

"It was rather curious to see how George Hardwick is breasting the rougher seas of Third Division football. However no sympathy need be wasted on Mr Hardwick. He is doing very nicely, thank you. On Saturday his play had a singularly detached air. He seemed to be in the game but not of it. Whatever routine moves he thought fit to make he seemed to draw instinctively from the vast stores of personal experience and memory. Shrewd positioning enabled him to obtain the maximum effect with the minimum effort. By his ability to think several moves ahead, and especially to anticipate his opponents' intentions, he could make his counter moves at walking pace. Here is another ripe for inclusion in the select band of strolling players."

Missing a number of games towards the end of the season made me realise that there was no substitute for playing. Having to watch from the sidelines, as my new club battled for promotion without me, did nothing for my nerves. I would never have believed that managing a football club could be so exacting. I certainly discovered aspects of my temperament I never knew existed.

For example, during our final few matches at Boundary Park I was unable to sit still on the bench. I had to stand on the steps of the players' tunnel racked by nervous tension, kicking every ball, until I was more exhausted than the players.

Those games were a tortuous, never ending, ordeal. The players and I had put so much effort into the season that it would have been an injustice if we had failed to gain the promotion we so richly deserved. That nail-biting experience certainly confirmed to me that playing is a darn sight easier than managing.

Although we had achieved promotion on the field of play, behind the scenes I was at odds with the board. To call it a board was something of a contradiction in terms because the fourteen Oldham directors at that time functioned more like an old gentleman's sherry club.

I was totally mystified by their reaction to our promotion success. The immediate priority for the club was naturally to retain our newly acquired Division Two status. But when I requested the finance to purchase the players to achieve that objective, the monetary assistance was not forthcoming.

I was personally bitterly disappointed with their attitude, particularly after all the hard work I'd put in. I felt I'd turned the club around almost single-handedly and believed that we were only a couple of younger "hungrier" players short of being able to comfortably hold our own in the new division. In fact those new faces were crucial if we were not to struggle the following season.

However the directors were completely unmoved. It was to be their lack of ambition which would cause our downfall the following season.

Ironically, while I was at loggerheads with the Oldham board I was fully aware that larger clubs, such as Stoke City and Bolton Wanderers, were closely monitoring my early managerial progress. Although that interest did not deflect me from continuing with the job that I'd started at Boundary Park, in hindsight, I possibly should have encouraged their advances. Unfortunately money management, and not player management, would dominate the rest of my Oldham career.

Despite the lack of support from the boardroom, I had to do what I could for the team. I had one ambition for the 1953/54 season and that was to consolidate our position in the Second

Division. I was confident that given a relatively injury free season we could adapt, even though stepping up just one league was going to be an immensely tough test of my team's limited ability.

My optimism, however, was totally misplaced.

There was no money available to strengthen the playing staff and with the average age of my second team only 18, we struggled from day one. We did not have a good enough or large enough squad to cope with occasional injuries. In fact we were firmly anchored to the foot of the table for most of the season.

We were inevitably relegated after conceding 89 goals, recording only eight wins and achieving a paltry 25 points from a season in which, because of the long term injuries I'd feared, we had to blood no less than six teenagers.

Remarkably, despite our hopeless position, and using thirty different players, we still managed to play some good football. But a comment from Everton manager Cliff Britton, who said that we were the best footballing side the Blues had played against since the war, was of no consolation.

After that disastrous season I realised there were some major drawbacks to being a player/manager, particularly with regard to running the rule over prospective new players.

Although my dual role gave me the element of control I'd desired, I was still first and foremost a player, and an integral part of the team. That situation meant any personal scouting missions at the weekend were impossible. So I had rely on the opinions of others, which I was loathe to do, especially as their assessment of a player's potential was sometimes at odds with mine.

Away from the pressures of the football pitch, some light relief was provided when I attended the wedding of Lancashire cricketer Bill Lawton and actress Dora Bryan on a snowy February Sunday afternoon at St Thomas's Church, Werneth. The snow was so deep near the church that the hundreds of shivering fans who had gathered to wish the couple well, warmed themselves by pushing the wedding cars through the drifts so they could attend the reception at the Greaves Arms Hotel.

Dora, who had grown up in Oldham and began her acting career in the local repertory company, eventually moved with Bill to London, where I frequently visited them at their home. In fact staying with the Lawtons for any length of time was like watching a who's who of the British theatre and cinema pass before your eyes.

Through my friendship with Bill and Dora I was privileged to meet, and escort to dinner, some of the most attractive leading ladies of the period including Kay Kendall, Sally Anne Howes, Shirley Eaton and Margaret Lockwood.

The monetary situation at Boundary Park did not improve at the beginning of the 1954/55 season. The chairman went on the record as saying that the financial position was far from strong. Again.

Apart from re-signing Don Travis from Chester for a nominal fee, I had to transfer players to provide the club with a much needed cash-flow and rely on raw young local talent. It was a situation with which I quickly became frustrated.

So did the fans. Attendances plummeted to under 5,000 after our relegation from the Second Division. During a difficult season, in which a 16 year old, Kenny Chaytor, made his debut, and Don Travis scored over 30 goals, we eventually finished in mid-table, which I thought was no mean achievement considering the mitigating financial constraints.

To supplement my player's fixed income at Oldham I was director of the Irish FA's summer coaching courses and periodically organised exhibition and charity matches in Northern Ireland.

On the return journey from one of those excursions in December 1954, the sea crossing became a most unpleasant and stomach churning experience.

Oldham's Harry McShane and I boarded the ferry at Belfast after our 5-3 victory in Distillery, and were due to arrive at Heysham, Lancashire, in the early hours of the morning.

That meant I was left with plenty of time to travel back to Oldham and attend the weekly directors' meeting at which the team for the forthcoming game was always chosen.

Unfortunately, during the Irish Sea crossing we encountered a storm which whipped up the sea. The ferry was unable to dock in port owing to the rough conditions. So the captain anchored offshore for over twelve hours until the winds abated.

Looking out of the cabin portholes all I could see were the giant waves battering the ship. The constant buffeting caused the vessel to roll and pitch violently in the swell, and I had to hang on for grim death to even stay in my bunk.

Anyone who has suffered from acute seasickness will know what an unpleasant 12 hours I spent trapped on board that ferry, and how relieved I was to reach dry land, albeit on rubbery legs.

Not surprisingly the club's financial situation did not improve as we approached the 1955/56 campaign. The chairman once again publicly attempted to rally the remaining hard core support, but they had become rather immune to the club constantly pleading poverty. Falling gates had hit the club hard, so in order to cut costs my retained list comprised of only 19 players, including five part-timers.

From my point of view the situation continued to be deeply frustrating and I realised I had to try something new to regain the interest of the supporters. I therefore endeavoured to introduce a more Continental style of football to the club. It was one which relied on the players interchanging their positions. It was a system of play which I later introduced to the Dutch FA, where it was christened Total Football.

The system, however, requires players of a certain ability level to make it work and my Oldham experiment was not a success. The only record we achieved was the club's highest number of draws in a season.

As the campaign was drawing to a close I took stock of my personal position and realised I had taken the club as far as I could. Oldham had no money to develop along the lines I wished them to go. Therefore I could no longer do my job effectively. I decided to resign my position in April 1956 and played my last game at Boundary Park against Wrexham.

At the time I commented to the local press:

"There is no ill feeling within the club. I have thoroughly enjoyed my spell with Athletic and have made a lot of good friends in Oldham."

With the passage of time I have not changed that viewpoint. I

146

believe I did all I could for the club within the financial restrictions I was working under. In fact I was probably too loyal. On reflection a move to a bigger club, after our promotion, would have been in my professional interest.

I thought, by and large, that the people of Oldham were marvellous during my time in charge and they generally gave me positive support, regardless of the team's results. They understood the fiscal position.

I particularly enjoyed attending the many local presentation evenings to which I was invited and making appearances at functions organised by bodies such as the Rotarians.

My family and I really felt part of the local community. But as my wife Joy commented at the time, after I'd faced an angry public meeting to try and explain the financial situation to the fans, it was about time to call it a day. I could see her point. I'd done as much as I could.

Over fifty years on I still have very fond memories of Oldham, and I was very honoured in 1995 to be seated at the top table for the dinner which commemorated the club's centenary.

The 1952/53 season is a year in my football career which I will always remember with great personal satisfaction. And I hope the more mature Boundary Park supporters retain the same fond memories of an outstanding promotion season.

· NINE ·
Working for Uncle Sam

Following my decision to leave Oldham, I did not have to wait very long for the new coaching offers to come rolling in. In fact I had two interesting offers from overseas. One came in August 1956, from the Cairo Football Club, which I declined because of the worsening political situation between Britain and Egypt.

The other was from Singapore. If I'd been single, I may have given the Asian position some serious thought. But with the well-being of my family to consider, uprooting them to the other side of the world was out of the question.

For a short period I worked for the Football Association as a staff coach at Loughborough College, alongside Joe Mercer. Then I received a call from the FA out of the blue, inviting me to attend a meeting in London. They informed me that I would find the agenda of some interest.

At Lancaster Gate I was rather surprised to find myself being introduced to three high powered American army officers. One of whom was the striking figure of General Bruce Clarke, Commander-in-Chief of the United States Forces in Germany.

Coming straight to the point, General Clarke explained that since the end of the Second World War a strong American military peacekeeping presence had been maintained in Germany, but unfortunately the bases housing the young GIs were experiencing dreadful discipline problems.

It was felt by the officers in charge that a lack of co-ordinated physical exercise, particularly for those too small for basketball or gridiron, was creating an atmosphere of deep frustration. As a result of their inactivity, many of the soldiers were becoming involved in aggressive incidents between themselves and the local young Germans.

In order to address the disruptive behaviour, it was thought a new focus was needed through which to channel all that pent up surplus energy.

The proposal on the table, therefore, was for me to devise from scratch, a structured coaching programme which would introduce the American servicemen to the delights of soccer.

I must admit I was quite taken by the idea. I had never imagined that I might one day be teaching football to the Yanks, but this was a completely new challenge and I was immediately taken by the opportunity for a change of environment. So I had no hesitation in accepting the position and, after making suitable arrangements for my family to stay in England, I flew from London to the United States 7th Army headquarters, which were situated in Stuttgart.

I was looking forward to getting my teeth into the job, but I had no idea what to expect. I must admit I walked into one a hell of set-up. In fact my lifestyle changed out of all recognition almost overnight.

As part of my contract I had at my personal disposal a six seater aircraft, a helicopter, my own staff car and driver - a great kid from the American deep south called Quincy Ponder - and a handsome pay cheque. To cap it all I was granted the honorary rank of full colonel, with living quarters to match my status. With the greatest respect to Oldham, it was a huge change from the circumstances of my last job!

General Bruce Clarke was very supportive, and I was responsible only to him. He was determined that every effort would be made to ensure that I could instigate my plans exactly as I wanted. He told me emphatically:

"If you have any problems George, I'll have their arses."

I cannot praise highly enough the encouragement I received from the Americans during my stay. I was given every possible assistance. They seemed to have faith in my ability to deliver what they required and I'm sure that I did not let them down.

The overall control of the project was my total responsibility and I revelled in the challenge. I was given *carte blanche* to organise the large scale and ambitious teaching programme. I was ably assisted in the implementation of my plans by five other first class British coaches including Johnny Spuhler, who had played with me at Middlesbrough, George Dick, John Ebby, Len Goulden and Frank Hill.

Although the living conditions were impressive, and the salary likewise, I must emphasise that the assignment was no relaxing holiday.

I worked a full eight hour day, five days week, and then drove back to my headquarters in Stuttgart, for course assessment sessions every Sunday morning. After lunch, in order to increase the American officers' awareness of game, I would take them to a German First Division match before travelling on to a new base to initiate the next training programme. It was a very hectic, but rewarding schedule.

I assigned myself, at the request of HQ Stuggart, to working specifically with the 7th Army troops. That took me, and my personal assistants, Lasik Besczy and Jacko Jacabuski, to bases in Frankfurt, Heidelberg, Kaiserslautern, Karslsruhe, Mannheim, Weisbaden, Ulm, Nuremburg, Wurzburg and Munich. The two lads were a tremendous help because they'd both played some football in Hungary and Poland before emigrating to the USA and joining the army.

The facilities on the bases were first class. They resembled miniature towns with cinemas, shops, luxurious accommodation blocks, schools and colleges, all serving the thousands of GIs and their families.

Initially we had no equipment with which to work and I had to beg and borrow as best I could. Eventually the sessions got under way when the English and German FA's kindly donated the balls, nets and goalposts.

We had plenty of open space at our disposal, but before the scheme could commence in earnest, I had to personally supervise the marking out of all the pitches, because nobody else knew how to do it. When it came to soccer there was a complete blank in the American consciousness.

We began the courses by teaching the American lads some very rudimentary football skills, such as control and passing, before gradually moving on to player positioning and elementary tactics.

Most of the boys adapted well to the game, displaying a great deal of enthusiasm and a surprisingly good level of skill. They did, it has to be said, encounter some difficulty understanding the basic rules, particularly what constituted an offside decision. But there again, English linesmen and referees are also still coming to terms with that law, so the young GIs were not alone in their confusion.

By the end of my stay I had established over 300 fully equipped teams who were regularly playing in leagues. In fact some of the American teams became so proficient in the game that they were permitted to join the minor German divisions.

That specific development, I thought, was a real achievement, considering part of the initial social remit of the coaching courses was to address the animosity between the GIs and the locals. It only goes to prove that football can be used as a common denominator to develop closer relationships between people from differing backgrounds.

In addition to the leagues, I organised an American Army Cup competition at battalion level, the final of which was played before a crowd of over 20,000 at the Mannhiem Stadium, with the German international referee, Herr Schmetzer, in control.

I remember playing myself in one of the earlier rounds of the tournament for a team predominantly comprised of soldiers belonging to the Army Medical Corps. They were unfortunately one of the weakest teams in the cup, but I figured that if I was injured, at least my treatment would have been quickly to hand. It would also be of the highest quality!

I shall always remember the American troops primarily for the enthusiastic way in which they embraced a game totally alien to their culture, and also for their overwhelming hospitality. Everywhere my fellow coaches and I went it was "open house", regardless of rank. From five star generals down to humble privates, the warmth of their welcome was marvellous and all encompassing. Frequently the breakfast menu included Alka-Seltzer.

When I left the American 7th Army I was presented with a beautiful clock and a pen and ink stand, the latter of which was engraved with these appreciative words: With the thanks of General Bruce Clark o/c US Forces in Europe.

· TEN ·

Going Dutch

The success of the American Airforce project, and the professional credibility I established as a result, enabled me to carefully select my next position.

I found myself being head-hunted for many of the vacant coaching jobs, including an unlikely approach from the Turkish FA, who wanted me to foster the development of football in their country.

Again, the interest from other nations was all very flattering. But the only other job I seriously considered, and eventually took, was with the Royal Netherlands Football Association.

In November 1956 I was invited to apply for the position of manager/coach to the Netherlands national team by Karel Lotsy, with whom I'd kept in close contact ever since the international match between England and Holland, at Huddersfield, in 1946.

A month later I was requested to give a demonstration of my coaching methods to officials representing the Netherlands FA at the Olympic Stadium, in Amsterdam.

I must have made quite an impression, because by the turn of the year I was not only appointed director of coaching and national team manager, but also had stored my furniture in England, and was living with my family in a glorious flat in The Hague, courtesy of the Dutch officials.

Within a couple of days of my appointment I was *en route* to Madrid, taking charge of an ageing Netherlands representative side, to face the strong Spanish national team.

Still playing international football was the experienced inside-forward, Faas Wilkes. Ten years previously we had been in

"Where's the soap?" The communal bath in the Ayresome Park dressing-room was a far cry from the individual facilities provided for the players at the state-of-the-art Cellnet Riverside Stadium.

Wearing our stylish training gear, England international Mick Fenton and I, welcome new signing, Andy Donaldson, to Ayresome Park, January 1949.

Referee George Reader, smartly attired in his blazer, watches Johnny Carey and I shake hands before the Great Britain v The Rest of Europe match at Hampden Park, Glasgow, May 1947, which was a personal milestone in my career.

As an FA staff coach I spent many enjoyable hours developing the skills of keen youngsters. Here Mickey Fenton and I supervise a demonstration of some basic techniques, at The Arthur Head School, Stockton-on-Tees.

Young Teesside lads crowd around Stan Matthews as he visits my sports shop in Linthorpe Road, Middlesbrough.

I'm presented with some lucky heather as I run out at Boundary Park for my
Oldham Athletic debut, November 1950.

A publicity snap taken to promote the new Oldham Athletic club badge,
which I helped to design.

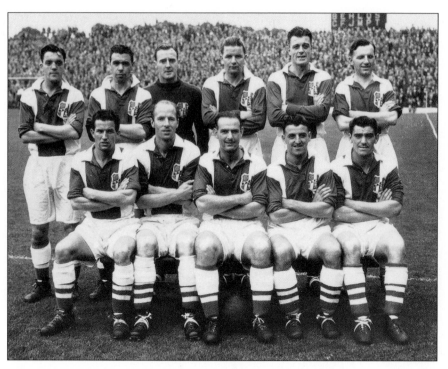

The Oldham Athletic team which I lead to the Third Division North Championship, in 1952/53. Back row: l-r Lowrie, Brook, Burnett, McKennan, Whyte, Smith. Front row: Munro, Gemmell, GH, Crawford, Ormond.

Local Oldham lads feel the strain, as I put them through a rigorous fitness session at Hollins Secondary School.

General Bruce Clarke, (centre), discusses with an FA colleague and myself, the implementation of a soccer coaching programme on the American 7th Army bases, in Germany.

Kaiserlautern, September 1956. Some of the first American GIs who attended the football clinics which I coordinated.

The steam rises as the Dutch national team realise their new director of coaching means business after stating his main priority was to raise their stamina and fitness levels.

My two sons, Andy, (left), and Mike studying hard while I was manager of PSV Eindhoven.

For nearly 40 years I conveyed my thoughts on the burning football issues of the day to the readers of both national and local newspapers.

Charity and benefit matches have always played an important part in my life. Here is the
Showbiz XI which played against my All Stars team at South Bank FC, Middlesbrough, and
included Billy Wright, David Frost, Wally Barnes, Tommy Steele and Harry Fowler.

Sunderland captain, Charlie Hurley, explaining the extent of an injury to me.
Unfortunately he spent too much time on the treatment table while I was at Roker Park.

Life after football. Here I'm representing Howst Ltd at a Tokyo business fair.

When we first met Jennifer was an air hostess
on a trans-Atlantic flight to America.

Jennifer and I pictured with our wedding guests. On my right is RAF friend, Stan Ballard.

Welcoming my horse, Young George, into the winner's enclosure at Redcar racecourse.

Pictured in Amsterdam with our great friends, Betty and Barrie Allum.

Guests at my surprise 75th birthday party, kindly organised by Ron Lester, and held at Ayresome Park, included left to right GH, Harry Bell, Johnny Spuhler, Wilf Mannion, Brian Clough, Geoff Walker, Alan Peacock, Bob Brady, Rolando Ugolini and Harold Shepherdson.

We may not have lasted very long together at Sunderland but Brian Clough has always kept in contact over the years. Here Cloughie is pictured with Jennifer and I in the Ayresome Park hospitality suite.

Good health! Bryan Robson visits the Blue Bell, in Middlesbrough, where the manager, Ron Darby (centre), has kindly dedicated part of the hotel's lounge to my football career.

George Hardwick has been a subject on many cigarette and trade cards.
(Above l-r) Godfrey Phillips -Turf Cigarettes, Sports Favourites - A. & J. Donaldson,
Sun Soccercards - Sun Newspaper.
(Below l-r) Stars of the Past - Richards Collection and Famous Footballers - Chix series 1.
(Cards courtesy of Harry Greenmon) (JW)

Wilf Mannion and I outside the gates of Ayresome Park, home of Middlesbrough FC, where we played together for over 13 years.

opposition, when Holland and the Rest of Europe were convincingly beaten by the England and Great Britain sides I'd captained.

Although the Dutch lads suffered a rather heavy defeat in Spain, their application and effort ensured they were far from disgraced. The game was also a useful exercise in enabling me to assess the standard and ability of the players with which I was expected to work.

It was obvious from the outset that a good deal of rebuilding needed to be done if the Dutch were to make any impact on the European footballing stage.

After watching the Spanish game, my initial priority was to dramatically increase the players' stamina levels. I therefore devised an intensive fitness programme to address that deficiency. Another pressing problem was that the majority of the side, although not lacking in technical ability, was comprised mainly of mature part-time players. It was crystal clear that an immediate influx of younger blood was required in order to implement any of the changes which I envisaged.

When I attended my first meeting with the Netherlands FA Council, to discuss my coaching plans, it was like travelling backwards in time. I found myself in a similar position to that which had stifled England manager Walter Winterbottom in the previous decade. The problem of blatant job interference by the administrators was strongly in evidence at the Netherlands FA Council.

It was patently obvious that the selection criteria applied to the national side was not based on a player's footballing ability, but on the influence exerted over the RNFA by particular powerful club presidents.

For example, at one selection meeting I was officially told that I must choose a certain player at outside-left, otherwise his omission would cause great offence to his club's officials.

From the outset, I made it plain that I was not happy with the selection procedures. I eventually settled for an uneasy compromise which enabled me to use my coaching ideas to redevelop the other Dutch representative sides, but relinquish some of my autonomy with regard to the national team.

For as long as I could remember I'd always had a clear vision of how, under ideal circumstances, I wanted the game to be played.

It was a system based on sound technical skills, using players who were both comfortable in possession, and had the ability to interchange positions when and where necessary during the course of the match.

I'd tentatively introduced the Total Football system at Oldham but, with no disrespect to the lads at Boundary Park, they lacked the level of technical ability needed to implement what I was trying to achieve. However, it was a different state of affairs in Holland, because there were so many young players with terrific ball playing talents. It was easy to adapt those skills to Total Football. So I set about instilling them with my ideas with great enthusiasm.

It turned out to be a great success, because strong foundations were laid for the future. Over the years I saw my original basic ideas adapted and modified by other Dutch coaches, before they finally evolved into a style of play which helped the Dutch national team reach consecutive World Cup Finals, in 1974 and 1978.

In the early days of my appointment I spent many hours travelling around Holland watching numerous games and assessing the promising young talent who I hoped would form the basis of my structured coaching programme.

From the resulting training sessions, I was able to select my own young Dutch B team to play against Germany, in Duisberg.

Prior to the game the Dutch press were extremely alarmed at the inexperienced team I'd selected, but I firmly believed that it was the only way for the standard of football in the country to progress. In the event the young lads did me proud and gained a creditable draw to emphasise that my coaching strategy was already developing along the right lines.

I also concentrated a good deal of my time working with the Dutch youth team, and in order to monitor the progress I was making, I arranged a game against England at Griffin Park, Brentford.

Again my team performed well, recording another promising draw, despite the efforts of a young man called Jimmy Greaves, who gave our defence a very testing time.

154

My optimism was further confirmed in a World Cup qualifying match, against Austria in Vienna, when the senior team's performance exactly replicated my pre-match tactical strategy.

During the first period we played some impressive controlled passing football, and by half-time led 2-0. However, our lack of experience at that level was exposed in the second half, when we were narrowly defeated in the closing stages after a dubious penalty awarded by Herr Schmezter, the referee who had officiated at the US Army Cup Final for me in Mannhiem.

Even the most partisan of Austrian supporters acknowledged that it was a refreshing performance from a country which previously had no pedigree on the international football stage.

The post-match reaction of the national press was very positive indeed. The Netherlands FA even rewarded the players and myself with a special financial bonus.

I felt my coaching methods had been vindicated, and they were further enhanced when I took a Dutch B team on a three match unbeaten Scandinavian tour which resulted in three convincing victories over Norway, Sweden and Denmark.

In June 1957, and with no imminent change to the RNFA committee's procedures in sight, I politely refused the offer of an extension to my contract. There was no animosity on either side. We just agreed to disagree on the policy governing the selection of the national team.

My resignation also took into consideration how slowly similar change had taken to implement in England, and I felt my personal position would only lead to professional frustration.

When the news of my resignation became common knowledge in Holland, I was immediately approached by Mr Philip Otten, the chairman of leading Dutch club, PSV Eindhoven, with an offer to become their chief coach and manager. It was an opportunity I had no hesitation in accepting. I loved the way of life in Holland, and the warmth and friendliness of the people, and I was certainly in no rush to quit the country. In any case, PSV were a large club with good potential, and there was fresh scope to put my coaching plans into operation.

The club certainly did not lack finance because its facilities were underwritten by the huge Phillips electrical corporation.

The company had invested heavily in a variety of sports centres in the local area, which provided a wide range of activities for the workforce and their families. The football section alone had over 700 registered members fielding 30 competitive teams each week, ranging from ten year old youngsters through to the senior side.

I found the PSV players individually more skillful and technically superior to the average British footballer, although they were not as physically aggressive. I felt that we would be a better all round side if I could introduce a bit of aggression. So, to add that bit of steel to the team, I signed fiery Welsh international winger Trevor Ford, with whom I'd had many a personal duel in the early part of his career, when he played at Aston Villa. He knew how to put himself about.

Trevor was a great talker on the pitch and often threatened to rearrange my "pretty" face during the course of a match. And, as I recall, he succeeded on one occasion, when I had to have six stitches inserted in a facial wound as the result of one particularly robust challenge from the Welshman.

The football facilities provided by Phillips were vastly superior to anything available in Britain at that time. Apart from a main stadium, the club boasted ten perfect full-size practice pitches, three of them floodlit, and a state-of-the art indoor hall, with full gym equipment. It was a marvellous set up.

On the whole, I had quite a successful season with PSV, finishing fifth in the league, and reaching the Netherlands FA Cup Final, where we were beaten.

I also achieved another ambition when I brought my PSV team to play against my old club, Middlesbrough, in March 1958, during Ayresome Park's first season of floodlit friendlies.

Unfortunately, as I remember, it was an extremely foggy night. The weather, however, failed to stop a certain centre-forward named Brian Clough from scoring a hat-trick, which he seemed to do with monotonous regularity in those days. The match ended in a 3-3 draw.

For personal reasons I was also very grateful for that trip to England because it was the last time I saw my dear father. He sadly died before I had the opportunity to return to live on Teesside.

Although I was offered an extension to my PSV contract, Joy and I decided, for the sake of Mike and Andy's education, that we would return to England where I'd endeavour to pursue a more regular career outside the game.

While I'd been working for the RNFA, both the lads had successfully attended the British Embassy School in The Hague. But when I took charge of PSV, there was no school available for Mike in Eindhoven, so he stayed behind with friends in the Dutch capital. It was not the most ideal of domestic arrangements.

So, at the end of the 1957/58 season, after two demanding years of coaching on the Continent, I returned with my family to Teesside.

I'm not going to pretend that it was an easy decision to make. In fact if the truth be known, it was the biggest professional mistake I made in my whole life. I not only sacrificed my growing reputation as an innovative coach, but also a salary and lifestyle which could never have been duplicated at that time in the English game.

But there are certain times when family priorities become of paramount importance, and should take precedence over all other personal considerations. Under the circumstances we felt it was the correct and appropriate course of action to take.

• ELEVEN •
Roker Choker

I was sad to see my football involvement on the Continent come to an end, but it was still good to be back in England again and meet up with many old friends. Joy and I eventually chose a new home in Hutton Rudby, North Yorkshire, and the whole family quickly settled in. Having made up my mind to sever my connections with football, it was my intention to turn a life long interest in cars into a career.

In order to gain some experience of the motor trade I joined an established local garage company called Martins. Selling cars was a completely different way of life to what I had been used to over the previous fifteen years, but I soon got my feet under the table and I believed that I could be successful in my new vocation.

However, football was in my blood. And, no matter how hard I tried to hide the fact, I was always only a phonecall away from being pulled back into the game which I loved so dearly. In fact I was happily managing the Martins site in Marton, Middlesbrough, when football, in the guise of Boro manager Bob Dennison, called again in August 1961.

Bob invited me to work as a part-time coach at Middlesbrough FC, taking over the running of the Northern Intermediate youth side. He wanted me to replace the departing Jimmy Gordon, the wonderfully conscientious and hard as nails wing-half, who had remained one of my closest ex-Boro colleagues. Jimmy had just left the Boro to join Blackburn Rovers as chief trainer.

That turned out to be a first step up the ladder for Jimmy, who later moved, with great success, on to the coaching staff at

Derby County and Nottingham Forest where he worked alongside two other former Boro stalwarts, Brian Clough and Peter Taylor, as they plundered vast amounts of silverware at home and abroad.

Before Bob Dennison's approach, I'd effectively been out of the professional game for over two years. Naturally I had continued to take a great interest and read as much information as I could on what was currently happening in the game. But my only real link was that I was writing weekly football articles for the Evening Gazette in Middlesbrough.

The opportunity to work with the Boro youngsters was very appealing and I was delighted to accept Bob's kind offer. It was marvellous to get involved with young players again and the role with the Boro rekindled my interest in coaching. In fact I thoroughly enjoyed myself running the Northern Intermediates and continued in that capacity with the club until Bob Dennision left in 1963.

The Boro first team was beginning to struggle in the Second Division at that time, but the club had some super kids on the way up. Many of the lads I worked with during that period, I'm glad to note, made their mark in the professional game. They included Frank Spraggon, Alec Smith, Des McPartland, Bobby Brass and the late Cyril Knowles. It was Cyril who was the pick of a good bunch because, after one outstanding season in the Middlesbrough first team, he was sold to Tottenham Hotspur and became an England international.

I loved working with those kids, but very soon I was back in football on a much bigger stage.

In November 1964, I was in the Roker Park press room, simply collecting information for my column, when my career was to take yet another twist. Sunderland's club secretary, George Crowe, called in to inform me that the chairman, Syd Collings, wished to speak to me.

As I sat down in the plush surroundings of the chairman's office, I automatically presumed he was about to reveal the name of the club's new managerial appointment. Sunderland had been without a manager since Alan Brown, who had taken Sunderland to promotion to the First Division, had left to take over the reins at Sheffield Wednesday. It was a bit of a scoop to be selected as the journalist who was exclusively invited into the chairman's office to be given the name of the new boss. I eagerly awaited to see who it was going to be. So, you could have knocked me down with a feather when, right out of the blue, Syd Collings offered the position to me. I was the main character in the exclusive story I'd hoped to scoop.

I'd been given no previous indication that my name was even under consideration for the vacant position. There was no formal interview process. Sunderland didn't want me to give them my CV, or try to explain why I was the right man for the job. The chairman simply said that the club would be pleased if I accepted the position. To say that I was taken aback by Mr Collings' offer was a complete understatement.

However it was not a bad job offer for a part-time journalist. Sunderland were a massive club and, better than that, they were based in my native North-east. I already knew a lot about the team, who had played some great football in winning promotion the previous season. I also realised that Sunderland were a club with massive potential. The possibilities were limitless.

Even so, it was an amazing offer considering my time away from first team management. No doubt I could have been forgiven for turning it down on the spot. However, being the sucker that I am, and unable to resist a challenge, I willingly took over the helm at Roker Park.

I certainly didn't walk into the job blindfolded. For a start, I knew I wasn't exactly Sunderland's first choice candidate. Originally there had been over eighty prospective applicants, and the job had already been rejected by numerous higher profile managers including Don Revie, Tommy Docherty and Bob Dennison. Many bigger fish than me had also been overlooked. But I had lost none of my self-belief and I felt certain that I could make a success of the job.

My reasons for returning to the heartaches of football management were nothing deeply philosophical. I'd had enough time to recharge my batteries and just wanted to be once again totally involved in the game that I'd loved ever since receiving my first football at the age of three.

My years as a player and a manager had supplemented a wealth of knowledge to my innate enthusiasm and I hoped to impart that experience to the Sunderland players.

Prior to appointment I'd also been working as representative in the oil industry and I needed a couple of days to sort out my personal affairs. However, once that was done, I was ready for the fray. In fact I could hardly wait.

Sunderland had been caught on the hop when Brown left them during the summer, after taking the club back to the First Division as runners-up to Leeds United.

Before my arrival, the club had been struggling on without a manager for over three months. It could hardly be described as the best way to try to settle into the relatively unknown but shark-infested territory of the First Division. Sunderland were, however, still attracting enormous support with crowds regularly approaching 50,000 and there were strong foundations on which to build.

The new campaign had started badly and steadily got worse. Due to pre-season injuries Sunderland had played 15 year old Derek Forster in goal, and seen Brian Clough's career finish after a failed three game comeback. They were near the foot of the First Division, having won only one of their first fifteen matches. The overall situation was not terminal, but they were certainly on the critical list. The immediate priority was to climb away from the bottom two and somehow retain their status amongst football's elite.

After formally accepting the position I quite happily stated in public that I would work without a contract and wanted to be judged at the end of the season on the results that I'd achieved. Taking everything into account, I thought it was the right and proper way to approach the job.

I did, however, shake hands on a gentleman's agreement which, as far as I was concerned, meant that if the team avoided relegation, I would be offered a long-term deal.

I was, and still am, a very trusting person and believe a gentleman's word is his bond. Although I had no written guarantee, I naively believed that the directors would honour the proposed arrangement.

The Sunderland team of that era had great potential, with players of the calibre of Jim Montgomery, Len Ashurst, Cec Irwin, Martin Harvey, Dickie Rooks, Jim McNab, Charlie Hurley, George Herd, Johnny Crossan, Harry Hood and George Mulhall on which to call. But the side patently lacked cohesion, pattern and direction.

By the end of the season, however, despite occasional problems with regard to some of my team selections, particularly around Easter, I had more than fulfilled my side of the bargain. The team gradually began to find their feet in the First Division, and slowly turned things around. At the end of the season we finished in a highly satisfactory fifteenth position, which was Sunderland's highest league placing since the Second World War.

Following the exciting FA Cup Final between Liverpool and Leeds, which the whole Sunderland squad attended as a reward for turning the fortunes of the club around, I was asked to attend a special board meeting at Roker Park to discuss my future.

During that meeting it was my intention to outline to the board my short-term plans. I hoped to build on the outstanding home form which had brought me ten victories, and was the bedrock of our survival. Away from home we needed to improve dramatically, and to achieve that objective I had in mind a few transfer targets who I felt would make Sunderland a more solid and determined team.

I was really excited about taking the club forward again and I fully expected the directors to honour our initial agreement and offer me a permanent contract.

However, before I had the chance to explain my intentions, I was hit by a bombshell. Syd Collings turned to me and said: "George....the directors have decided not to retain your services."

For a moment I was totally speechless. I struggled to absorb the enormity of what he'd said to me. After only 168 days in the job, despite achieving the First Division survival which the directors had required, I was about to be shown the door. I had delivered my side of the bargain, yet the Sunderland directors refused to honour their part. I was completely devastated and disillusioned.

The official club statement issued to the press regarding the decision was blunt, concise, and to the point:

"The temporary arrangement made by the board with Mr George Hardwick ended on May 1, 1965, and is not being renewed."

That economical one liner was the only public comment ever made by the club on my position. I felt, as did many of the supporters and local journalists at the time, that it did them no credit.

When I gathered my jumbled senses and asked for a further clarification of the board's decision, the reasons given for my sudden dismissal were rather obscure and contrived. It all seemed to hinge around my style of management. The board had the impression that I was too hard on the players, and far too familiar with the press.

I had to agree I was very demanding of the players, because at that time the Sunderland first team was underachieving. There were a lot of good players who were not doing themselves justice. There was absolutely no doubt at all that a tough regime had to be implemented to get results. But the very fact that I saved the club from relegation surely vindicated my methods.

The incident to which they were probably referring happened at Elland Road in January, after a 2-1 defeat by Leeds United. I publicly lashed my players in post-match newspaper interviews, before I'd criticised them face to face.

Granted, the game was played on a tricky, icy surface which was not conducive to good football. But on the day it was a gutless showing, lacking in both passion and determination and I was not prepared to accept it. It was not good enough for me, it was not good enough for the directors and it certainly was not good enough for the supporters.

As a manager, defeat is always hard to take, but it can be a little more bearable if your team has given 100%, and you lose to the better outfit. In that match, however, the effort was minimal and I was angry. I personally felt let down.

Headlines in the press told the fans not to be misled by the closeness of the scoreline because it was Sunderland's:

"Biggest hammering in years."

This was a clear vindication that I had not personally misread the situation. The players just did not perform on the day. In fact it was only the inspired performance of goalkeeper Sandy

McLaughlin which prevented Leeds from registering a cricket score.

The move to publicly speak my mind was cold and calculated. I questioned the players' professionalism and dedication. I wanted them to read my outspoken reaction and then dwell on it for a few days. But above all, I wanted to hurt their pride because the thousands of loyal supporters deserved much better from their team.

As a result of that critical outburst, I achieved more in one weekend than I could ever have hoped to accomplish in a month of tongue lashings. The team proceeded to win six out of their next nine matches, including a 1-0 victory over the champions of that season, Manchester United.

The only defence I can offer for my actions was that I had to find short cuts to improve the team's performance. Division Two was looming perilously close, and I had no time to attend to the normal civil courtesies in order to obtain the necessary results. Drastic circumstances need drastic measures to bring about solutions. It was a battle for top flight survival, which I eventually won, so, as far as I was concerned the ends justified the means. I have no regrets about my actions.

Other factors which may have contributed to my downfall were my dealings with the club captain and the first choice goalkeeper.

Charlie Hurley was one of the most popular Sunderland players of all time. In fact he is still revered on Wearside to this day. But I upset his adoring fan club when I dropped him over the Easter period.

The simple truth was that Charlie had a shocker of a game in the 2-1 home defeat on Good Friday, against Wolves. It was not what I expected from him. This was an opinion which was shared by the press who commented:

"Hurley had his worst game in years."

Charlie never got to grips with the Wanderers' centre-forward, Hugh McIlmoyle, who was given the freedom of Roker Park. As a result, the team received the slow handclap for their indifferent performance.

Managers have to take unpopular decisions from time to time, and during my stay at Roker Park Charlie Hurley spent far too many matchdays on the treatment table. I'd be very surprised if he played in more than half the league matches under my management. Even when he did play, he struggled to find his form in the system I was playing. I could not accept that I had to play the club's star players if they were not doing themselves justice on the pitch. Nobody was bigger than the club and I had to select the side which I felt was best equipped to do the job on the day.

The Jim Montgomery situation was slightly different because he'd been injured before I was appointed. As a result, his competent understudy, Sandy McLaughlin, had taken over between the sticks. Sandy did not let me down, so for the majority of the season I continued with him as my first choice goalkeeper. It was my belief that Sandy deserved to stay in the side as long as he was playing well and doing everything that was expected from him. In fact it would have been grossly unfair to leave him out.

Failing to win back his No. 1 position was frustrating for Monty and I can understand any player's disappointment at being left out of the side. However, Monty's reaction at failing to regain his place was to submit a formal transfer request towards the end of the season. Whether the possibility of losing such a popular local player had some influence on the board's decision to release me I cannot say. However, I still stand strongly by the plain fact that, ultimately, the preservation of the club's status was more important than the feelings of, or for, individual players. Obviously I wanted Monty to stay because he was a very good goalkeeper. But I do not regret the way I handled either of those lads.

With regard to the press familiarity, I would stoutly defend that accusation. It was vital at that critical juncture that positive stories about Sunderland FC appeared in the newspapers. It was important not only to lift the morale of the players, but also the supporters, who were fast becoming disillusioned with the team's position.

To achieve that objective I had to make sure that the reporters who came to the ground for information were provided with refreshments, and received a full daily briefing from me updating current events. As a public relations exercise it cost the club next to nothing, and I considered it a worthwhile use of my time. I knew what information I could give to the press, and what I could not. There was never a case of me having released any stories to the newspapers which were private club matters.

To say that I was not satisfied with the board's waffling reasons for my dismissal would be an understatement. So I stood my ground and asked if any of them was man enough to give me the real reason why they were dispensing with my services. Not surprisingly gazes were averted, and a stony silence descended on the room.

As a parting shot I left the meeting by informing them: "If you don't need me, I'm as sure as hell I don't need you."

I'm certain, however, that one of the real reasons for my dismissal was my close association with Brian Clough.

Before I'd arrived at Roker Park, Cloughie had suffered a career-ending knee ligament injury. It followed a collision with Bury goalkeeper, Chris Harker, at Roker Park, on Boxing Day, 1962.

For such a dedicated player, who was used to scoring over 40 goals a season, it was a personal tragedy. On his own admission, Brian became bitter and very difficult to live with, particularly when he saw players of lesser ability still turning out for the Sunderland first team.

Brian's life was in a state of flux and limbo. I could empathise with his predicament because I too had gone through the same mental trauma some twenty years previously. The future suddenly becomes uncertain and that uncertainty slowly begins to eat at you, creating insecurity and self-doubt.

Brian also had a major problem. The only job he knew was football. Nothing else. He had no trade to fall back on. But what he did possess in great abundance was a deep-rooted love of the game. Whatever people think or say about him as a person, Brian's innate passion for football can never be called into question.

When I took charge of Sunderland, Cloughie was hanging around the place like a miserable and persistent North Sea fret. His much heralded comeback had failed, and although he was training to keep himself physically fit, he had no focus in his life. But I was determined to give him one.

I called Brian into my office and told him that I had a job for him. I informed him that he was going to work for me training the youth players. It was heart-warming to see Brian's positive and immediate reaction. He jumped at the chance, just as I knew he would. The appreciation was written all over his face as he warmly put his arm around my shoulder and said: "You'll do for me boss."

I wasted no time in getting him started and enrolled Cloughie on an FA coaching course at Durham, so he could obtain the necessary formal qualifications.

Talk about start as you mean to go on. Apparently, during the two week session at Durham, he made his presence heard and even questioned the teaching methods of the FA's Director of Coaching, Charles Hughes.

Once he'd qualified, I appointed Brian youth team manager, and under his enthusiastic guidance the performances of the young lads took an immediate turn for the better. In fact they did so well that they reached the final stages of the FA Youth Cup.

However, I had known from the start that Brian's appointment was not going to be a popular one in the boardroom. In fact I didn't immediately tell the directors about my plans for Brian. When I was finally forced to mention his name at the next board meeting, their reaction was one of controlled anger.

It was obvious they didn't want Cloughie on the coaching staff. In fact they would have preferred to have him out of the club altogether. So when I suggested my long-term objective, which was to appoint him as my right-hand man with the first team, I thought some of the directors were going to have seizures.

However, giving Brian that initial job was like leading a horse to water. Cloughie was an absolute natural. His immediate success with the youth team made him realise he could coach. Not only that, he realised that he was very good at it. He had the personality to motivate the lads who, in turn, respected his playing ability. He thrived on the added responsibility of the new challenge, and was keen to learn and bring in new ideas to improve the kids even further. In fact Brian began to adopt some of the training methods I'd preached in Holland.

Out went the monotonous drudgery of stamina training, and in came small enjoyable games of five-a-side focussing on improving the players' technical abilities.

Despite Brian's success, the undercurrent of anti-Clough feeling continued to emanate from the boardroom. We all knew, that at times, Brian could be his own worst enemy. He often voiced his forthright opinions at inopportune moments. Diplomacy was not his forte. But I had the distinct impression that the directors were not prepared to take into account the great job that he was doing for the club and still wanted him out of Roker Park altogether.

I'll never know what might have happened if I had been allowed to stay in the job as manager of Sunderland Football Club. Obviously my working relationship with Cloughie came to an abrupt end when I was not offered a permanent contract. Brian was apparently informed by the new manager, Ian McColl, that the directors wouldn't be too pleased if he stayed. Charming. Cash in on the insurance money you've received for an injured player and then discard him. Very caring. The whole sorry situation left me feeling sick in the pit of my stomach.

Whether the directors saw our burgeoning partnership as a long-term threat I can only speculate. All I can say is that I had a clear plan of how I wanted the club to progress, and utilising Brian's talents would have been an integral part of that development plan.

Brian was revered by all the supporters, as the attendance of 31,000 at his testimonial match underlined. Possibly the board felt it was going to be very difficult to work with two such determined characters, I simply don't know. However, whether through intent or accident, it's hard to believe that the best interests of the club and its devoted supporters had been put first in this matter.

When I was told, despite all my concerted efforts to save the club from the relegation trapdoor, that my services were no longer required I was deeply shocked. So were the majority of the fans, because many of them wrote letters to me disassociating themselves with the directors' decision. There was a widely held belief among the supporters that I'd been given a raw deal.

Most congratulated me for keeping Sunderland in the First Division. Others applauded the dignified way with which I had conducted myself during the course of the numerous television and radio interviews I gave after being relieved of my duties.

For their kind words and many letters of encouragement I was very grateful, and the following extract outlines the sentiments which were being expressed on my behalf:

"Mr Hardwick, I would like to say you are a gentleman and a true sportsman. After hearing your comments on TV I'm afraid I wouldn't have been so polite and genuine as you were.

"The ordinary men and women who frequent Roker Park are bitterly ashamed and disappointed that you haven't been allowed to finish what you started, and I hope whatever happens, you will take the best wishes of the people of Sunderland for the service you have given to the football club."

The decision of the Sunderland directors sickened me, and apart from an 18 month part-time stint with Northern Premier League club Gateshead, I effectively retired from professional football management the day I walked out of the Roker Park boardroom.

In my opinion the Sunderland directors missed a great opportunity to have an ambitious management team which was a rare amalgam of youth and experience. Who knows what may have happened to the club if our association had been given a chance to develop? You only have to examine Brian Clough's managerial record working in another partnership, to provoke a debate on that subject. I honestly believe that, together, we could have brought real, and hopefully lasting, success to Sunderland.

Unfortunately Sunderland never went on to achieve that lasting success in the First Division and, in fact, they have never properly established themselves in the top flight since then. Yet Cloughie went on to win national and European championships with Derby County and Nottingham Forest. Facts which are worthy of reflection on Wearside, I feel.

A short while after leaving Sunderland I received a call from Ernie Ord, the chairman of perennial Fourth Division strugglers Hartlepools United. Mr Ord was keen for me to become the manager at the Victoria Ground.

Although I declined his genuine invitation, I did suggest the name of a young man who I thought had real managerial potential. That name was Brian Clough.

While I have no wish to take any credit for Brian's later success, I am glad to note that Mr Ord followed up my sound advice and gave Cloughie the opportunity to confidently place his foot on the ladder to managerial greatness.

The final irony with regard to my experience at Roker Park was that most of the football world knew I was working without a contract. So, once it was obvious, in April 1965, that Sunderland would be playing First Division football the following season, I was approached by other clubs with a number of tempting job offers, but I politely turned them all down.

At the time I stated in the Sunderland Echo, when the rumourmongering about my possible departure first hit the streets, that:

"I was convinced all along that we would not be relegated and I have planned for a long stay with Sunderland."

Well it only goes to show just how wrong you can be!

• TWELVE •
Gateshead – the last hurrah

After my sobering experience with the Sunderland board of directors, I made a determined effort to finish with football management altogether. I knew that I could be very successful as a football manager. But I wondered whether I could cope with a similar disappointment in the future. So I decided to concentrate all of my efforts on building a new career for myself in industry.

I worked successfully for a structural steel company called JPG, who were based in Skinningrove, North Yorkshire, supervising contracts for a new terminal building at Heathrow Airport and a Glaxo Factory at Barnard Castle, in County Durham.

Everything was going according to plan and I never considered another return to football - until I received a telephone call from Gateshead FC chairman, Mr J. Bowman.

At that time in the late 1960s, south of the Tyne, there were great forces for social change led by the borough's dynamic mayor, Councillor Bill Collighan. He steadfastly believed that the prestige of the town and the success of the football club could be interlinked.

He had a staunch ally at Redheugh Park in Bob Tulip, grandson of the redoubtable Bill Tulip, who had been part of the furniture during Gateshead's days as a League club. Bob also felt, that far from being doomed, the club had a valuable role to play in the town's regeneration.

When I was offered the part-time position as manager, Gateshead FC was in one hell of a financial mess. Many of the senior officers were threatening to resign over the club's dire predicament. In addition, there was constant friction with the local council about the decaying condition of the stadium, which was in urgent need of redevelopment.

With a population of over 100,000 people, the town had enormous crowd potential. So, once again, I just couldn't resist the challenge, and eventually accepted the job at Redheugh Park.

Gateshead, a club which had held League status only a decade previously, was long overdue a revival. One of the major problems to rejuvenation, however, was its close proximity to Newcastle United and Sunderland. Both of these major clubs were regularly drawing large crowds in excess of 40,000 at that time.

When I commenced my managerial duties in May 1968, the club had just joined the newly formed Northern Premier League. In the days before the Conference, this was possibly the strongest non-league division in the country. I was very optimistic that I could revive the club's fortunes, but I knew that any success would hinge on gaining the whole-hearted backing of local councillors, and the remaining hardcore support.

To raise the club's profile within the area I helped to organise a public meeting in July. It was attended by the newly elected mayor, Charles Rymans, and the leading officers of the club including Mr J Bowman, Mr E Pringle and Mr C Jefferson.

The overall response to the meeting was at best lukewarm, with less than 100 people in attendance. But it was a start, and I outlined my plans to the assembled gathering.

The most positive outcome of the meeting came when two 12 year old boys, Paul Jopling and Jeffrey Brown, volunteered their services to undertake any task which would benefit the club. It was the type of response I was looking for. But it needed to be multiplied at least a thousand fold, if the club was going to make any significant progress.

At the time of my appointment at Gateshead, I made comparisons of potential with Scarborough FC. They were also a non-League club at that time, but were regularly attracting crowds of over 2,000, and had an extremely active development association providing them with a useful supplementary income.

In order to survive, I felt that Gateshead needed to emulate Scarborough's administrative organisation and build up a solid base of support within the local community. I was convinced that if they adopted the same strategies as the seaside club, advances could be made at Redheugh Park, despite the rival attractions of their big city neighbours.

How prophetic those comparisons I made over thirty years ago turned out to be, as Scarborough deservedly achieved, and have maintained, their League status.

The first few months of the 1968/69 season were very difficult for Gateshead Football Club. As well as trying to combine a day job with my part-time football duties, I was also endeavouring to develop a style of play suitable to the experience and talents of the lads on the staff.

By the turn of the year we were struggling badly at the bottom of the league, with only ten points. It was taking time to put things right within the team. Then, suddenly, everything that I was hoping to achieve clicked into place. We won half a dozen games in a row and started to make steady progress up the NPL table.

The improvement was based on the strong defensive performances of George Siddle who was, in my opinion, the best centre-half in the league. The youngsters I'd blooded at the start of the season also found their feet, particularly John Gilmore and Gerry Coyne, who began attracting the attention of League clubs.

The usually dormant local press, not known for openly supporting the team, suddenly rekindled its interest and began to cover our matches in greater depth. Positive headlines like: *"The Great Revival of Gateshead FC,"* *"Gateshead on a crest of a wave"* and *"Gateshead boys shine in fine win"* began appearing in the previously reticent Gateshead Post.

The spirit and confidence within the whole club grew appreciably at that time. The players even took on the responsibility of producing their own programme for our home matches.

I also felt that I was making significant headway on the pitch because we were gaining a reputation within the league as a good footballing side.

By March 1969 we had climbed to a respectable mid-table position, losing only once in ten games. But, disappointingly, the crowd figures never rose above the usual few hundred loyal souls. The meagre attendances were baffling, not only for me but also for the players, who were by then on an excellent run of results and deserved a better level of support.

During that period of improvement even the Gateshead Post asked of its readers:

"Surely the team's performances on this showing are worthy of much better support." And *"Gateshead in championship form. Pity the success has escaped the Gateshead public's notice."*

I couldn't have agreed more with those sentiments because the club was having its best season in years.

However, despite all my optimism and initial success, I have to honestly say that the job at Redheugh Park was an exacting and physically draining struggle from the beginning.

The root of the problem was that the club could not generate or sustain enough cash-flow, either through the turnstiles, or via an efficiently run development fund. Money was desperately needed to renovate the poor changing facilities and the structure of a stadium which was in a crumbling state of disrepair. The financial situation had not been helped by the loss of valuable revenue following the cessation of greyhound racing a couple of years earlier.

The beginning of the 1969/70 season saw us undefeated in our first three games, including a fine victory over the previous league champions, Macclesfield Town.

Unfortunately the continuing lack of finance created a vicious circle of events when the players' wages went unpaid. This was a huge disappointment to me, but a bitter blow for many of the lads who relied heavily on the money to supplement their incomes. It was only natural, therefore, that the players began to drift away to more stable clubs, where payment was guaranteed.

The mass exodus of players meant we fielded teams often containing many amateurs, and I had to utilise raw local talent in order to fulfil our fixtures. I did, it must emphasised, receive the total backing of the new enthusiastic chairman, Bob Tulip, and we endeavoured to find ways of tackling the on-going cash crisis.

The chairman himself publicly displayed his commitment to the club by participating in a series of sponsored walks. But try as he might to gain the support of the local business community, his sterling efforts met with an apathetic response from the town's commercial sector. They just didn't seem to care what happened to the town's football team, and that was undoubtedly the crux of the problem.

We even adopted a short-lived free admission policy for children but, although the gate often doubled in size, the wanton vandalism which the kids caused to the buildings and equipment during the course of a game, often meant that the repair bills exceeded the gate receipts.

In a last ditch attempt to raise some much needed capital, I contacted Brian Clough and Joe Harvey to arrange challenge matches against Derby County and Newcastle United in the New Year.

Brian's reaction was marvellous. However, even though he sent his full first team for the game, the attendance at Redheugh Park barely topped 1,600. It raised a little over £200. Bob Tulip and I were deeply shocked at the lack of interest shown by the Gateshead public to the fund raising ideas.

In late January the financial situation became even more critical. Then, after a sequence of events that would have tested the patience of any manager - because they had nothing to do with the team's performances on the pitch - even I came to the conclusion that enough was enough.

Firstly the club couldn't afford to heat the water for the showers, due to major problems with the Dickensian plumbing system. Then our dilapidated mini-coach had two punctures on the way to an away match. This resulted in us arriving 15 minutes late for the kick-off, despite changing in the bus. Finally, I cringed with embarrassment when we had to borrow a set of socks from Darlington FC to complete our kit for a North-eastern Cup tie.

By that time I'd been working long hours for no pay. I was flogging a dead horse and eventually had to admit defeat because my own health was beginning to suffer.

A few months previously I'd collapsed at work and spent a period in North Ormesby Hospital, near Middlesbrough, undergoing tests for a heart condition. Naturally my family and friends were very concerned about my health and didn't want me to do anything stressful which might aggravate the problem.

So, with great reluctance, I resigned my position at Gateshead in February 1970 in the face of impossible odds.

The ailing club did not have the resources to bring about the necessary improvements and went on to finish at the foot of the Northern Premier League. As a result, they had to apply for re-election, which was denied them, and they spent the next season playing in the Midland League.

On reflection, I don't think I could have done any more under the trying circumstances. This fact was graciously recognized by Bob Tulip who said: "I am deeply sorry at George Hardwick's decision and cannot praise his efforts too highly."

It was a very frustrating conclusion to a promising first season and in some ways mirrored my predicament at Oldham Athletic. When things were successful, the potential on the pitch was there for all to see. But any aspirations which I held to develop either team were quickly overtaken by the financial problems both clubs experienced.

I am glad to see that in more recent times the future of Gateshead FC seems to be a little more secure since they moved to the town's international athletics stadium, and I wish them well.

• THIRTEEN •

A heartening degree of success

Following my retirement from football management my private life underwent a period of considerable transition during which time my mother, bless her, passed away and I remarried.

I met my beloved second wife Jennifer purely by chance on a Trans-Atlantic air flight in 1967. She was the highly efficient chief stewardess on an aircraft chartered by my good friend Don Robinson, to take members of the Newcastle-based Northern Sporting Club to Las Vegas for a world heavyweight title fight.

Despite the obvious domestic upheaval that our relationship initially caused, I have remained in contact with my sons Mike and Andy, both of whom live with their families in the Scarborough area. Mike served for a number of years in the Royal Air Force, before taking up an administrative position with the police, while Andy has pursued a successful career in education.

Once I'd left Gateshead FC, despite receiving many interesting offers, I was never again tempted back into football management. In fact I consciously diverted all my energy into a variety of business interests and media work.

However, although I thoroughly enjoyed my work outside football as chairman and director of several successful companies including: JPG Industrial Engineering, Howst Ltd, Clemcrest Engineering, George Hardwick Inspection Ltd, AGA International Ltd and Teesside Training and Technology Centre Ltd, I never became totally detached from the game I love because I knew I'd only suffer from acute withdrawal symptoms.

I was also fortunate that as a former England captain my

opinions on contemporary football were continually canvassed by all sections of the media. That constant level of involvement led me not only to pursue a parallel part-time career in journalism but also to work in television and local radio as a programme editor, presenter, commentator and summariser for Tyne Tees, Granada, and the BBC.

As I've always enjoyed meeting people and exchanging views on a wide range of sporting issues of the day, working in the media was ideally suited to my personality, and gave me a great deal of satisfaction.

Another sporting passion with which I became more closely involved in the 1980s was horse racing. In fact I became the proud owner of three racehorses, Hit the Town, Young George, and Red George. It was the fulfilment of a long held ambition that began as youngster after riding my grandparents' ponies in Lingdale.

Trained by Colin Tinkler at Maltby in North Yorkshire, they won numerous competitive handicap races at Redcar, Newcastle and Perth giving me a great deal of enjoyment into the bargain.

Since quitting football one of the most emotional moments of my life came in May, 1983, when Middlesbrough Football Club kindly arranged a testimonial match for Wilf Mannion and myself at Ayresome Park. It had been hoped to stage a game on our behalf at an earlier date, but the board of directors, for some reason, constantly denied us their consent and prevented the match from taking place.

I don't intend to rake over old ground or discuss the political in-fighting which caused that sad situation to arise, but I do feel, even now, that it is important to thank the organising committee for their hard work. It was undoubtedly due to the persistent efforts of Owen Willoughby, Terry Jackson, Tony Bentley and Roland Connelly that the original idea for a match eventually became a reality.

Mike McCullagh, the chairman of the club at the time, must also take a great deal of the credit for breaking the previous boardroom intransigence which enabled the game to be played at the famous old stadium.

Finally, with regard to the testimonial match itself, I'd like to thank the England players and their team manager from that era, Bobby Robson, for giving up their time. But most of all, I must emphasise just how much I greatly appreciated the support of the thousands of loyal fans who made it such a splendid evening.

Over the years there's been a natural tendency, due to peoples' ever changing personal circumstances, for me to lose touch with some of the close friends I'd made during my football career. However, in February, 1995, I was able to totally indulge myself during a wonderful afternoon of nostalgia.

Thanks to the hardworking efforts of a family friend, Ron Lester, a surprise 75th birthday party was held in my honour at Ayresome Park, prior to the home league match with Reading.

The function was attended by many former Boro and England colleagues including Wilf Mannion, Mick Fenton, Harry Bell, Johnny Spuhler, Geoff Walker, Alan Peacock, Rolando Ugolini, Harold Shepherdson and Brian Clough.

In what was Middlesbrough's last season at Ayresome Park, it was quite fitting that I should celebrate such a personal milestone at the ground, which, over the years, had been my spiritual home.

Although I have to be honest and say that the closure of Ayresome Park was tinged with sadness, I knew, only too well, that in order for the club to progress and compete with the best, they had to move from the cramped urban terraced streets which surrounded Ayresome Park, to the new state-of-the-art Cellnet Riverside Stadium.

When the ambitious relocation plan was announced I applauded their decisiveness because it was the first time in my life that I'd ever known Middlesbrough FC contemplate such a large-scale expansion.

On the day of the final match against Luton Town in April, 1995, attended by many ex-Boro players, the importance of the game to that season's promotion push tended to overshadow the fact that the curtain was slowly descending on 92 years of the town's football heritage.

It was only some months later, when I attended the auction

held to dispose of the ground's fixtures and fittings, that I finally accepted it was the end of an era.

The turf, which had been graced by so many of the game's greatest players, was receiving its last rites and would soon be replaced by the grass verges of a modern housing estate.

As I strolled around the eerie remnants of a once proud stadium, I felt as though a close and dear friend had passed away. It was a truly emotional experience. I repeat, I wholly understood the reasons for the ground's closure, but it didn't make the loss any easier to bear.

The positive attitude adopted by Middlesbrough's new regime is certainly a refreshing change from the financial strictures, which were imposed in my day. Then, the frugal club secretary, Herbert Glasper, made me account for every single penny of my expense claim.

I do wish my old club well in the immediate future, and trust that they will eventually find the right blend of players to wear the famous blood-red shirt with pride and reward the faithful Boro supporters with their first major trophy. It's long, long, long overdue. I only hope it happens in my lifetime.

When I began playing football over 75 years ago in the East Cleveland village of Lingdale, like most schoolboys, I constantly dreamed about wearing the hallowed white shirt of England emblazoned with the rampant three lions. Later, I was extremely fortunate not only to fulfil that youthful ambition but also to achieve the ultimate accolade and captain my country on 13 consecutive occasions at full international level.

One of the most memorable of those matches was against Scotland in April, 1947. To lead the national side out of the famous Wembley tunnel into the full glare of a packed stadium was one of the highlights of my whole playing career. There was something almost magical and spiritually uplifting about the atmosphere generated inside the old stadium. It was like having an extra player on your side. I loved the place. I only wish I could have played there more often.

So, when in early 1999 I was contacted by Adrian Bevington of the Football Association's media relations department, asking me to be their guest of honour at the England v France international match on February 10, I had no hesitation in accepting their kind invitation. The match would also provide me with one last opportunity to see the old twin towers as I remembered them before a new stadium, fit for the 21st Century, takes their place.

I must give credit where it is due, because the organisation of the whole trip was superb. Initially, Jennifer and I were flown on the British Midland shuttle from Teesside Airport to Heathrow, from where an official car took us to the exclusive Whites Hotel in the heart of the capital. Following a relaxing afternoon, we were then driven in style to Wembley for a pre-match buffet with the FA's hierarchy including, the chairman Geoff Thompson and the flamboyant ex-sports minister Tony Banks.

Tony, as we all know, is a life-long Chelsea supporter and during our conversation he told me how his late father had watched me play for the Blues at Stamford Bridge throughout the Second World War. I was one of his favourite players and he'd always wanted to meet me. I was only sorry I couldn't oblige.

Everything about the evening was timed to perfection and 15 minutes before kick-off I was escorted down on to the pitch to be introduced to the teams. Apparently, as I was shaking hands with the players, one of the TV commentators noticed I was wearing a sheepskin coat and wondered if it was on loan from John Motson. Very sarcastic. And no it wasn't.

To actually stand on the Wembley turf after half a century brought back to me all those international matches of Matthews constantly mesmerising the full back, Finney's incisive wing play, Mannion's silky skills, Swifty's commanding goalkeeping and Lawton's fearless heading ability. The memories were still so vivid in my mind. It felt like only yesterday.

Jennifer and I watched the match from the comfort of the royal box with our legs wrapped in warm blankets against the chill winter air. Unfortunately, the game wasn't as entertaining as the preliminaries and England were rather comfortably beaten 2-0 by the World Champions. However, the French Ambassador, Monsieur Jean Gueguinou, did his best to keep us all amused because as France began to dominate the possession he continually apologised to everyone for the score.

Following the match we returned to our hotel with some of the FA officials for supper. That pleasant repast concluded what had been a very hectic but most enjoyable day.

After breakfast, there was another wonderful surprise when the FA gave us the exclusive use of a chauffeur driven car for the day. Our first pre-arranged port of call was to sign copies of my autobiography at the Sportspages Bookshop in Charing Cross, where I must say the lads made Jennifer and myself most welcome. Then, before flying home, we rounded off our trip to the capital with my first visit to Madam Tussauds Waxworks. When we saw the size of the queues outside the popular attraction we were very grateful that our tickets were ready and waiting at reception, courtesy of the FA, otherwise we would have stood for hours waiting to get in.

On reflection, although the whole Wembley visit was an absolutely tremendous nostalgic experience, it was tinged with certain amount of regret that I'd not had the opportunity to captain Middlesbrough in an FA Cup Final. Somehow I think the great Boro servants of my era like Wilf Mannion, Mickey Fenton, Rolando Ugolini, Ronnie Dicks, Jimmy Gordon and Johnny Spuhler would have relished such an occasion. Sadly, it wasn't to be, but I was glad that I'd paid one last visit to the old stadium before it was demolished to make way for its modern day counterpart. In terms of atmosphere and memories the new ground certainly has a lot to live up to.

Jennifer and I had a superb few days and I would like to formally thank Adrian Bevington and the Football Association for their generous hospitality. You did us proud.

A large percentage of my original autobiography was devoted to the happy time I spent in the 1950s across the Pennines in Lancashire, managing Oldham Athletic. Although at the time I made many good friends, I was still astounded by how many Latics supporters bought my book from their club shop. In fact the overall sales figures were so encouraging that I was invited back to my old stamping ground in March, 1999, for a signing session prior to the match with Bournemouth.

It was a memorable afternoon returning to Boundary Park to

meet so many old friends and supporters, most of whom could remember, in great detail, many of the matches and incidents I had long since forgotten.

It's only when you spend some time reminiscing with the "real" fans that you realise the impact that you've had on their lives and how much they cherish their own personal footballing memories. We as ex-players, should never forget the people who ultimately paid our wages.

At half-time I was introduced to the crowd on the pitch and received a very warm reception indeed. Some wag even called out for me to get my boots on as Oldham were losing at the interval. I must admit I was tempted.

Despite the full-time score, Latics eventually lost 2-0, I enjoyed my return to Lancashire immensely and I'd like to thank Ian Stott and his fellow directors for their generous hospitality towards Jennifer and myself. I really felt at home because the traditional ground and its surroundings hadn't changed a great deal since my day. The floodlights still dominate the skyline and Boundary Park can't escape those penetrating wintry elements that blow down from the moors. I do, however, wish my old club every success in the future.

For some considerable time I have suffered from the heart condition angina, but I've always managed to keep it under control with regular medication and by adopting a sensible lifestyle.

However, during 1999 the attacks became more frequent and severe, resulting in my specialist, Dr De Belder, suggesting I should enter South Cleveland Hospital for an angioplast, which he hoped would widen the blood vessels around my heart.

Unfortunately, following some rigorous tests it was discovered that my arteries were too narrow for this procedure to be effective and the only alternative treatment was a bypass operation.

I must admit it was a great emotional shock to the system when the seriousness of my condition was revealed to Jennifer and myself. In fact, the long-term prospects were not at all good. I was told in no uncertain terms that if the bypass procedure was not undertaken immediately there would be a fair chance I'd not see another Christmas. In other words there was no time to lose.

So, on July 5, 1999, leading heart surgeon Dr Wallace, performed a double heart bypass operation which I'm pleased to say was a complete success. And thanks to the wonderful medical care I received at the South Cleveland Hospital cardiology unit I was able to return home on July 16. Physically, the procedure was very demanding indeed, followed as it was shortly afterwards by urgent prostrate surgery. Consequently, I lost over a stone in weight and had to make further changes to my lifestyle.

During this period poor Jennifer was under real pressure because not only was she attending to me but to her mother, Florence, who had also been taken into South Cleveland hospital at the same time. How she coped only she knows because her stressful daily routine seemed to entail constantly moving from one part of the hospital to another.

Unfortunately, after a brief stay in Nunthorpe Hall Residential Home, Florence returned to the hospital following a stroke and sadly died, aged 96, on August 14. Jennifer was of course totally devastated and it was a very trying time indeed. For both of us.

Following the bereavement we decided, after much consideration, to move into Florence's house in Yarm.

Initially I have to admit that I found the move a real wrench. Having lived in rural Stokesley for the best part of 26 years I missed the picturesque views of the moors and the small town community where I knew most of the residents and the shopkeepers by name. Gradually, however, I've managed to adapt to the change of surroundings and as long as I can have a periodic fix of the North Yorkshire countryside, I'm fine.

I have to be honest, I naively thought that once the bypass operation was completed my heart problems would be eradicated. However, this optimism was shown to be totally misplaced when, a year later, after feeling unwell at home, I was rushed by paramedics to North Tees Hospital cardiology department with a suspected heart attack.

After four days of intensive tests, during which time I was continually connected to a heart monitor, the overall conclusion drawn by my specialist, Dr Smith, was that I'd probably suffered a mild stroke.

Although my speech was initially affected there was, thank goodness, no apparent paralysis. However, the incident has certainly caused my memory to be less sharp but, with Jennifer's constant care, and the support of my many friends, I am, once again, living my life to the full.

Throughout my football career I was very fortunate to receive numerous awards including the proudest day of my professional life when I received official notification from the Football Association that I'd been chosen to captain my country.

More recently, however, one of the most satisfying awards I've received was an honourary Master of Arts degree from Teesside University in November, 1999.

There's always something very special about accepting an award from organisations and institutions within your hometown area. It's as if the local population are conferring their own formal appreciation and final seal of approval for your efforts.

The ceremony, held at Middlesbrough Town Hall, was a very grand affair and followed a night of pampering at the four star Crathorne Hall Hotel where our hosts even catered for our poodle, Toffee.

For the official presentation, conducted by the rector of the university, former European Commissioner, Leon Brittan, I wore a very appropriate resplendent red gown and mortarboard. I felt like a real academic.

What an immensely proud day it was for me to receive my honourary degree alongside such luminaries as the noted Oxford academic Dr David Butler, the very respected local hospice fundraiser Mary Butterwick, popular ballet dancer Wayne Sleep, and world renowned sculptors Claes Oldenburg and Coosje van Bruggen who created the monumental "Bottle of Notes" which soars over 35 feet in the centre of Middlesbrough.

I'd also like to thank Graham Henderson from the university staff for officially proposing me for the award and for the kind comments contained in his speech about my career. What a final conclusion to an education which began at Lingdale Council School over three quarters of a century ago.

Following the ceremony, all the recipients were invited to

return to the university refectory for a celebratory lunch at which I was joined by many of my closest friends.

A nother major milestone in my life was achieved on February 2, 2000, when I was 80. The surprises began the day before when Jennifer arrived home with an unexpected "treat" in the form of our close friend Betty Allum who had flown in from Holland especially for the occasion.

My birthday started bright and early with a visit from the Evening Gazette's photographer, Doug Moody, who called to take a picture of Jennifer and myself sharing a "champagne" breakfast.

Following a relaxing time answering a constant stream of phone calls from well-wishers, and reading the many cards and goodwill messages which had arrived in the post, I'd expected to round off the day with a quiet evening meal at the Blue Bell Hotel in Acklam with Jennifer and Betty. However, when we arrived at reception, instead of entering the restaurant, I was directed into the aperitif bar to be greeted by my two sons Mike and Andy and 34 of our closest friends. What a surprise! I was then whisked upstairs to the function room, which bears my name, The Hardwick Suite, for a delicious five course meal. The evening, secretly organised by Jennifer and the hotel general manager Ron Darby had apparently been planned for weeks. I must admit I never suspected a thing, and the unexpected element made it such a wonderful evening in the company of those people who have played such a major part in my life.

As it turned out I must have had one of the longest 80th birthdays on record because, unbeknown to me, my editor John Wilson, had approached Middlesbrough FC about the possibility of formally marking the occasion with a celebratory football dinner. And I'm pleased to say my former club readily agreed.

The function, for which I must thank our good friend the club's commercial director Graham Fordy, was held in one of the hospitality suites at the Riverside Stadium on February 18 and was an absolute nostalgic delight. It generated so much local interest that it was even covered by regional and Boro television.

The evening was planned to perfection and contained

everything I enjoy most in life (well almost) - good food, great company, music performed by the Redcar and District Amateur Operatic Society, and a hilarious comedian. There were over 200 guests in attendance including, I'm pleased to say, many ex-Boro players like Johnny Spuhler, Tom Blenkinsopp, Ray Yeoman, Eric McMordie, Frank Spraggon and John Craggs. The only major disappointment was that my old pal Wilf Mannion was too ill to attend. The guest of honour, however, was a little known local lad made good called Brian Clough.

Brian and I had worked together when I was manager of Sunderland for a brief period in 1965. On this particular night he made a highly personal speech acknowledging that all he'd achieved in football management over the years could be traced back to the time I persuaded him to take up coaching after his playing career was prematurely ended through a knee ligament injury. It was very kind of Brian to be so complimentary and acknowledge my initial contribution which instigated his outstanding managerial career. Humility is a facet of his character that he rarely reveals in public and to my mind it is still one of life's great mysteries why he was never appointed England manager.

Again what a delightful evening of entertainment, and all for my benefit. I was beginning to feel very spoilt and slightly embarrassed by all the attention.

• FOURTEEN •

Dear friends remembered

O ver the last couple of years some of my most dear friends have unfortunately passed away and I couldn't possibly update this book without mentioning the very important part played in my life by Wilf Mannion, Stanley Matthews, Stan Cullis, Willie Maddren and Stan Ballard.

W ilf Mannion was blessed with so much natural ability that he often found the game ridiculously easy. He was undoubtedly one of the most gifted and talented players of his generation, or for that matter, any generation. We both grew up in South Bank and played against each other on numerous occasions for St Peters and East End. Unfortunately, like most of us at that time Wilf lost the prime years of his career due to the Second World War and while on active service endured great physical hardship. It was therefore to his credit that he managed to resume his career after the hostilities ceased and regain the level of performance that deservedly won him many international accolades.

However, I've always had a nagging doubt in the back of my mind that Wilf believed he'd underachieved throughout his playing career. Like me, he never won a major trophy in the game and when the right opportunities arose to move to a much bigger club than Middlesbrough, and there were many, the board at Ayresome Park were unwilling to sanction his transfer. That intransigence, which was fully discussed earlier in Chapter Five, certainly soured his relationship with the directors who had denied him the chance to display his skills at a more fashionable and high profile club.

Undoubtedly, when he was in the mood, Wilf Mannion was a footballing genius with few equals. He was a player who could win a game on his own. I'll never forget his two-goal virtuoso performance for Great Britain against the Rest of Europe at Hampden Park in May, 1947, or his deft ball juggling antics to impress his fiancée, Bernadette, against Blackpool in November, 1947.

In private, Wilf was a very modest man. His favourite pastime was to indulge in a quiet game of billiards out of the limelight, and although he had been ill for some time, his passing still came as a great shock to me as our careers had been intertwined for so many years.

On the day of his funeral the cortege paid a poignant and appropriate visit to the site of the old Ayresome Park ground where thousands of Wilf's adoring fans turned out to pay their last respects to the "Golden Boy." The packed service, held at the Catholic Cathedral, Coulby Newham, was attended by many past and present Boro players together with representatives from other clubs, and was a fitting tribute to a much loved local football legend.

A few months after Wilf's death Middlesbrough Football Club paid him the ultimate compliment when they commissioned a special bronze statue of South Bank's finest, sculptured by Tom Maley.

As a lifelong friend I was extremely proud to perform the unveiling ceremony in October, 2000, on the main concourse outside the Riverside Stadium. It was quite an emotional moment for both the Mannion family and me when I removed the drapes to reveal the impressive eight foot likeness which captured Wilf, as I remember him, in free-flowing action.

Knowing Wilf as I did, he would probably have been rather embarrassed by all the fuss but proud to think that his memory will live on forever. We'll all miss him.

When I heard of Stan Matthews' death in February, 2000, I was really taken aback because out of all the players of my generation I would have to say that "The Wizard of the Dribble" was the fittest man I'd ever seen.

Stan was one of the first players to consciously monitor his diet and he trained harder than anyone I've ever known. He played at the highest level for more than 30 years with great distinction and consistency for Stoke City, Blackpool and England. In 1957 he was even acclaimed as European Footballer of the Year at the age of 42, and was still playing first team football for Stoke when he was 50. In later years he even told me that, on reflection, he thought he'd quit too soon! I knew exactly what he meant. There's nothing to compare with actually playing the game. Once you've retired, the withdrawal symptoms stay with you for the rest of your life. As I mentioned earlier in the book, playing football was like taking a drug. The craving just never goes away. It's totally addictive. I can assure you that neither managing nor spectating is any kind of substitute for being out there on pitch.

I was fortunate to be Stan's England captain just after the Second World War and we were great friends. He had the ability to literally mesmerise the opposition full back with his trickery. I know, I was on the receiving end on more than one occasion during games between Blackpool and Middlesbrough. I also lost count of the number of international goals his unselfish wing play created for Tommy Lawton and his club colleague Stan Mortensen. However, Stan, for all his abundant talent, was a very modest, humble and unassuming man. He tried to evade all the media commotion that, even in our day, surrounded football, preferring to stay out of the spotlight. I have no doubt, like Wilf Mannion, he would have been highly embarrassed by the massive outpouring of affection for him on the day of his funeral in Stoke. Tens of thousands of people lined the route as the cortege slowly wound its way through the terraced streets where he had grown up in the Potteries.

Stan was given a marvellous and highly emotional send off at St Peter's Church by officials and players from every era including, Sir Tom Finney, Nat Lofthouse, Sir Bobby and Jack Charlton, Gordon Banks and Jimmy Armfield.

The service, which Jennifer and I attended, was a deeply moving experience full of wonderful tributes, which spoke volumes for how much Stan was revered throughout the football world. Overall, the occasion was a credit to the city of Stoke and befitting someone who will always have a special place in the nation's footballing heart.

Stan Cullis was the first England captain I played under when I made my international debut in a wartime game against Wales at Nottingham in 1941. From the outset I must say his confident demeanour and leadership skills made quite an impression on me. He led by example and frowned upon the use of foul language to encourage his team-mates. He was a winner and no matter how difficult a game became he would keep driving his team on. You never dreamed that an international match would be lost with Stan as the captain.

Although during his distinguished career he gained something of a tough tackling reputation he was by no means a one-dimensional player. He was not only one of the best attacking centre-halves of my era but also a cultured defender who calmly intercepted the wayward pass and utilised the ball constructively. In Stan's eyes to needlessly concede possession to the opposition was almost a sin.

Stan was, in my opinion, the complete defender. Unfortunately like me, due to the Second World War, he was only awarded a dozen official caps when he actually represented his country on more than 30 occasions.

Stan's name was synonymous with Wolverhampton Wanderers for more than 30 years, the team he captained and later managed with great success, winning both the FA Cup and the League Championship. By the mid 1950s he was also an innovative coach believing that the technical ability of our players would be improved by playing floodlit European games against Russian and Hungarian opposition. That opinion was contrary to the rather staid position adopted by the FA's hierarchy who, at that time, despite England's 6-3 Wembley mauling by Puskas and Co in 1953, saw nothing to be gained from entering into European competition. Cullis disagreed with that introverted approach and proved the game's officials were out of touch when sell-out floodlit matches, against Honved and Spartak Moscow, captivated the Wolves supporters.

Although Stan had gained something of a reputation as a strict disciplinarian who believed that his players were also representing the whole town as well as the club, he did have a dry sense of humour.

Apparently, after one dismal Wolves performance he locked the players in the changing room and gave them a real dressing down. The 12th man, obviously pleased not to have been on the park that afternoon, and thinking he was excluded from the verbal tirade, started sniggering. Stan noticed his light-hearted reaction and said, "You!!!" "What are you sniggering at? You're so good you couldn't even get into this wretched team." What a brilliant put down.

Stan's funeral in March, 2001, organised by the Wolves Former Players Association, was held in the idyllic Costwold village of Colwall, near Malvern. It was attended by many of the games leading officials and ex-players including Doug Ellis, Bert Williams, Norman Deeley, Ron Flowers, Bill Slater, Peter Broadbent, John Richards and Steve Bull.

Stan Cullis was a fine man. Admired by everybody who knew him. In a world where moral values have tended to become eroded, Stan stood out as a man of principle. He will be sadly missed.

The death of Billngham-born Willie Maddren at the age of 49 from Motor Neurone Disease was nothing more than a tragedy. I'd watched him play as a youngster and knew instinctively that he would easily make the grade as a professional.

Although initially given his Ayresome Park debut as a forward by Stan Anderson, Willie later switched with great success to central defence and became one of the lynchpins of Jack Charlton's record breaking 1973/74 Second Division Championship winning side.

During this period there was a widely held belief that Willie was one of the finest players never to be capped by England at full international level. That was an opinion with which I fully concur. In fact to emphasise the point, when I was working for the local media I always remember an interview given by Kevin Keegan before Liverpool's FA Cup quarter final with Middlesbrough at fortress Anfield in 1977.

When asked about the Reds' Cuptie prospects, the former England captain replied, "It all depends on whether Willie Maddren is fit to play."

That revealing answer, from such a great player as Keegan, highlights better than anything I could say about the high level of professional esteem in which Willie Maddren was held within the game. The mere inference that a club of Liverpool's stature felt Willie's presence in the Boro line-up could have a crucial bearing on the final outcome of such a critical match gives us a significant insight into the admiration his peers had for Willie's ability.

Another important attribute worthy of mention is that I also believe, following the premature end of his playing career in the late 1970s through injury, Willie displayed a natural talent for coaching. If only he had been able to work in more favourable circumstances I'm certain he would have proved himself to be an effective manager. However, he rarely had the opportunity to fully utilise his ability because of the general malaise at Middlesbrough FC during the mid 1980s. I don't care how good a coach you are, without the necessary financial resources to improve the standard of your playing staff you are very unlikely to succeed. I know, I found myself in a similar position to Willie all those years ago at Oldham Athletic.

Once Willie publicly announced he was suffering from MND I greatly admired his determination to battle bravely against the debilitating illness for a number of years and, together with his devoted wife Hilary, raise thousands of pounds for the fund set up in his name. It is also to the credit of Middlesbrough Football Club that the Education Centre at the Riverside Stadium bears his name. It is a fitting epitaph to one of the finest local footballers of the modern era.

Although the Second World War was a shocking experience it was also a period of great camaraderie when lasting and deep friendships were forged. I was stationed at RAF Eastchurch on the Isle of Sheppey and it was there that I met Stan Ballard.

Stan had been a first class athlete in his time and had joined the services as a PE instructor. There are some people you meet with whom you are able to form an instant rapport. You're on the same wavelength. Stan was one of those people. We went everywhere together. In fact we became so close that he was the best man at my first wedding and also attended the ceremony when I later married Jennifer.

Halfway through the war, while I was playing football to entertain the troops, Stan joined the elite special forces and following the D-day landings in 1944 was secretly dropped behind enemy lines as part of a covert operational unit.

When the hostilities ceased Stan enrolled at the London School of Art before eventually opening his own successful business as a commercial artist, working for many established companies like catalogue firm Freemans.

Once he'd retired he moved into portrait work and began accepting important commissions, undertaking work for many famous people including Nick Faldo and Muhammad Ali. He even spent endless unpaid hours restoring a water-damaged scroll listing all my wartime appearances for England, which I thought, was beyond repair. Thanks to Stan's painstaking work it now hangs proudly in a prominent position in our hall at home.

Over the years Stan and I always kept in touch either through visits, phone calls or Christmas cards. Unfortunately, I hadn't seen him for nearly six years when out of the blue his son, Toby rang to say that his father was seriously ill. From what Toby told us it was obvious that Stan's condition was very grave indeed so Jennifer and I decided to pay him a visit at his home in Bexley, Kent. Although it was great to see him again, and we chatted about old times, he was obviously very weak.

I'm sad to say that not long after our visit he passed away and with him went another happy chapter in my own life.

· FIFTEEN ·

Freedom of the Borough

In my own eyes I was a footballer who always made the very best of his ability. But when you mix that ability with good communication skills and a fierce determination to succeed, you probably have the answer as to why I captained every team I played in. That said, it was still a very pleasant surprise indeed when in May, 2000, I received official notification from the Football League that I was to be acknowledged as one of the 100 greatest players of the last century at a special dinner in London. It was quite an honour, I'm sure you'll agree. Not only for me but also for Middlesbrough FC because Wilf Mannion and George Camsell were also featured on the list plus many other players with Boro connections like the first £1000 player Alf Common and former Ayresome Park manager David Jack.

As usual the travel arrangements to the capital were excellent. Jennifer and I caught the shuttle from Teesside to Heathrow from where we were taken by official car to the London Hilton, which, conveniently, was also the venue for the function.

The star-studded "Legends" dinner turned out to be quite an auspicious occasion. It was covered by the national media and during the course of the evening I was introduced on stage to the invited audience together with many of the country's greatest players such as Sir Tom Finney, Jimmy Greaves, Nat Lofthouse, Sir Bobby Charlton, John Charles, Denis Law, Alan Shearer and Sir Geoff Hurst.

Unfortunately, some of the gloss was taken off an otherwise marvellous evening when I noticed that my photograph was missing from the official portrait gallery. Due to an oversight my name had been inadvertently placed under a picture of Stan Mortensen by mistake.

Although I later received a profuse apology from the organisers it was rather disappointing that their research was flawed, particularly for such an important and unique commemorative occasion.

One of the pleasures of attending a function like the "Legends" dinner is the opportunity it provides to renew old acquaintances and friendships. At the Hilton Hotel I was pleased to once again meet Beryl Franklin.

Beryl is the widow of my ex-England team-mate and great pal Neil Franklin and I had not seen her for some years. During the evening Jennifer and I arranged to visit her the following month in Tiptree, Essex where we spent a very pleasant day recounting the highlights of Neil's outstanding club and international career.

On the same short break we also called in to see a man who was certainly one of the greatest influences on my professional life, Walter Winterbottom.

Walter became England's first team manager immediately after the Second World War and to this day I have no doubt that he was instrumental in my appointment as England captain in 1946. Our professional relationship was built on mutual respect and this understanding ensured a fine team spirit throughout the time I was leading the national side.

Walter was a man for whom I had the greatest admiration. It was the implementation of his original ideas immediately after the war, which helped establish a nationwide network of coaches to improve the game at grass roots level. That farsighted innovation was quite revolutionary in its day and set down the coaching blueprint for many years to come.

I had not seen Sir Walter, as he is now, for many years. But following enquiries kindly made on my behalf by Graham Fordy of Middlesbrough Football Club I was able to meet him at his home in Cranleigh, Surrey. I found Walter, who is about five years older than me, to be in good health and mentally still very sharp indeed. His wife, Lady Anne, prepared us a lovely lunch, before we spent an engrossing afternoon chatting over old times.

I've often been asked during interviews to name my most vivid football memory. Without sidestepping the issue, because I enjoyed every last second of my playing career, I find it very difficult to be so selective. For example making my debut for Middlesbrough and scoring an own goal after 60 seconds in front of your own supporters certainly made an early impression. Being appointed captain of the Boro, Oldham, England and Great Britain for the first time were undoubtedly some of the other highpoints. But if I was really pressed to choose my favourite, I'd have to plump for the day I led England to their 10-0 win over Portugal in May, 1947.

Many people say you should never live in the past. I wholeheartedly agree with that sentiment but that shouldn't stop you from occasionally looking back with pleasure at the happy times, which in my case, were spent playing the greatest game in the world.

So, when Jennifer and I booked a holiday cruise in September, 2000, I noticed that one of the ports of call on the itinerary was the beautiful Iberian city of Lisbon, which, coincidentally, was the scene of that England great victory.

At this juncture let me say that I never wanted to go on a cruise. Being held "captive" on board a ship has never really appealed to me. However, after some gentle persuasion from Jennifer, I must say my experience on the luxurious liner, Arcadia, changed my opinion completely. What a fantastic time we had. In fact we enjoyed the holiday so much we intend to book other cruises in the future.

When a friend, Ian Wright, heard that Lisbon was on our itinerary he suggested it would provide the perfect opportunity for me to revisit the National Stadium where the match was played and took it upon himself to make all the necessary arrangements.

I must say Ian did a splendid job. Not only did he organise the whole visit through the Portuguese FA but also waiting at the ground when I arrived was the right winger I'd marked all those years ago, Jesus Correia. What a surprise! We recognised each other immediately and through an interpreter he joked that he still had the bruises where I'd kicked him.

What a heart-warming day it turned out to be. The stadium had obviously been upgraded since I played there over half a century ago but, in general, it still looked the same, brilliant white in colour, and a vast open bowl. Just for a fleeting moment as I looked out over the ground I could see in mind's eye those great England players who I captained on that momentous afternoon, Wilf Mannion, Neil Franklin, Billy Wright, Frank Swift, Stanley Matthews, Tommy Lawton, Stan Mortensen and Tom Finney subjecting the opposition to a footballing masterclass. In fact the Portuguese team were so embarrassed about the emphatic final scoreline that they failed to turn up for the formal evening banquet.

To commemorate my visit, the Portuguese FA kindly presented me with a replica shirt and Jesus gave me a watch after which we were royally entertained to a splendid meal at a nearby restaurant. Finally, to round off the perfect trip, we travelled to the nearby resort of Estoril where the England squad were based prior to the game.

As I stood on the sun kissed promenade outside Europe's largest casino where, I seem to remember, one or two of the lads lost more than a few escudos, it was hard to believe that it all happened over half a century ago. Could somebody please tell me where all the time has gone?

One of the positive benefits of living in such a closely-knit community as Teesside is that Jennifer and I regularly receive requests from a wide variety of different organisations to attend their functions. I can tell you at my age I'm very grateful to be remembered, and those kind invites make for a very full social calendar.

One such invitation, in October, 2000, was to the launch of a superb new local book called Teesside's Sporting Greats. The publication, written and produced by my editor, Billingham-born John Wilson, and the Evening Gazette's Chief Sports Writer, Eric Paylor, is an impressive celebration of the areas sporting achievement throughout the last century. To even be included in such a prestigious publication was very pleasing indeed but I must admit I had no idea that I would be in such exalted company.

Being fully immersed in football all my life I'd forgotten that our area had produced so many outstanding international sportsmen and women in such a wide range of activities. For example Olympic, Paralymic and Commonwealth medallists like athletes Willie Applegarth, and Ken Churchill, swimmer Jack Hatfield, hockey player Michael Walford, cyclists Chris Newton and Paul Curran and bowls expert Norma Shaw. As well as a host of famous rugby, football and cricket internationals like Rory Underwood, Tim Williamson, Wilf Mannion, Mick Fenton, Brian Clough, Alan Peacock, Bobby Smith, Gary Pallister, Harry Makepeace, Geoff Cook and Bill Athey. The book quite simply contains *the* definitive roll of local sporting honour.

The dinner itself, held at the Marton Hotel and Country Club in Middlesbrough, was attended by many of the book's celebrities and their families. It was a thoroughly enlightening evening, with each of us receiving a complimentary copy of the book before being interviewed by local media personalities Gordon Cox and Alastair Brownlee.

The 95 detailed biographies contained in the book, coupled with the hundreds of archive photographs, were a real eye opener and I would heartily recommend this meticulously researched publication to anybody interested in local sporting history.

Throughout my career I believe I played with, and against, many of the greatest players of all time such as Stanley Matthews, Tom Finney, Tommy Lawton, Joe Mercer, Stan Mortensen, Wilf Mannion, Billy Wright and Frank Swift. The list is endless. In recent years there has been a resurgent interest in their careers and as a consequence the football memorabilia market has grown accordingly. Avid collectors are purchasing a wide variety of items such as medals, shirts, caps, cigarette cards and programmes relating to specific teams and individuals. Established auction houses now have football only sales and the price of material is steadily rising as demand increases.

Over the last few years I've been a client advisor to a well-known auction house and this position has enabled me not only to help ex-professionals with the sale of their memorabilia but also to meet players from other eras. One such player was

Frenchman Raymond Kopa who played for Real Madrid in the late 1950s and was voted one of the players of the tournament during the 1958 World Cup in Sweden.

Initially, a business colleague had organised for Jennifer and I to fly from Stansted to meet Raymond and his wife for lunch in the French town of Angiere. Following the meal the Kopas kindly invited us back to their magnificent house where we watched a specially compiled video of his career. I must admit I'd forgotten what a great player he'd been. Capped 45 times by France, triple European Cup winner, European Footballer of the Year in 1958 and in a recent poll voted the third best French player of all time behind Zidane and Platini.

As we watched the tape with interest, Raymond began to show us his fine collection of medals. These mementoes however, were only the tip of the iceberg because stored around the house were hundreds of other items including, plaques, cups pennants, autographed photos, programmes, tickets, shirts and trophies, all relating to Raymond's outstanding career. The total amount of material was astounding. I don't think I've ever seen so much quality memorabilia belonging to an individual player in one place.

Having seen the extent of the collection we advised Raymond to have it valued. This he did, and was amazed to find its true market value.

Eventually, Raymond decided to sell the material at auction and leave the money to his children. Those who viewed the sale acknowledged it to have been one of the finest collections of football memorabilia ever assembled and I was only too happy to be of assistance.

The game of football thrives on the memories of both players and supporters. Even now, after all these years, being able to recall with ex-colleagues and fans the great matches and teams in which I played during my career still gives me the utmost pleasure.

As the fluctuating fortunes of a football club are gradually absorbed into a town's folklore, the detailed preservation of that history is essential.

Thankfully, many officials, who after all are only the temporary custodians of a club on behalf of the fans, have now recognised the importance of their football heritage and are beginning to exhibit collections of memorabilia in purpose built museums so that supporters of all generations can relive and share past experiences.

One of the finest examples of this expanding trend can be seen at Old Trafford where Manchester United have created a quite stunning exhibition of silverware and memorabilia charting their illustrious history. Jennifer and I were fortunate to have a private tour of the museum and stadium from Warren Bradley and I was extremely impressed by the whole layout.

I know that United are not universally popular within the game, but you cannot ignore their outstanding achievements, particularly under the guidance of my old friend Sir Matt Busby and Sir Alex Ferguson. So for the football enthusiast the exhibition is certainly well worth a visit.

A football club should be founded on, and proud of, its history and tradition. That's why I feel the achievements of the players, who for more than 125 years dedicated all or part of their professional careers to further the cause of Middlesbrough FC, require some form of permanent recognition.

I'm justly proud that one of the hospitality lounges at the BT Cellnet Riverside Stadium bears my name. But I must stress that I was only part of a team, both at club and international level. There are many other lads who also deserve a similar lasting acknowledgement of their Boro careers. It would be good to know that in the near future these concerns were being addressed.

Over the years I've always thought that I could tell when Jennifer was being secretive. But in November, 2000, even my powers of detection evaded me when she organised a visit to the Riverside Stadium for myself and three of our friends.

The itinerary began with the stadium tour and was to be followed by lunch in one of the hospitality suites. However, as we reached the reception area there appeared to be an abrupt change of plan. Without warning we suddenly took a detour outside, on to the concourse.

As we emerged from the main entrance I became aware of a

smiling crowd of friends, officials and media people. At this stage in the proceedings I still had no idea what was beginning to unfold.

I was then greeted by the club's Chief Executive, Keith Lamb, who walked with me towards the centre of the concourse, where the statue of my old pal Wilf Mannion is situated. For some reason Keith asked me to step forward and face the gathered throng before he proceeded to summarise my football career. I must say he was so complimentary I didn't recognise myself.

At this juncture I was still totally unaware what was happening and when he handed me a chord and invited me to pull it, I just blindly carried out his instructions.

As I tugged, a white drape cascaded down to the ground revealing, on a raised plinth, a towering sculpture of yours truly. What a shock! I was left speechless. I couldn't believe how easily I'd been hoodwinked. How Jennifer had managed to keep the arrangements from me I will never know because apparently they were broadcast over the local radio and had also appeared in the Evening Gazette. I must have been the only person on Teesside who was totally kept in the dark about the unveiling.

The statue was absolutely first class. I must say that North-eastern based sculptor, Keith Maddison, certainly did a grand job and I owe him a deep debt of gratitude for creating such a perfect likeness. It captures George Hardwick in his prime. Just how I would like all the Boro supporters to remember me.

Now that I've had time to recover from the shock of the occasion it's rather humbling to think that you mean so much to the people of your hometown for them to preserve your memory for posterity. My grateful thanks are due to Steve Gibson, the chairman of Middlesbrough FC, and to all the club's officials who made this wonderful tribute possible.

Is it just my imagination or as you get older does your birthday appear to come round much more quickly? I must admit it didn't seem like 12 months since I was celebrating reaching the ripe old age of 80 with that splendid evening at the Riverside Stadium, but here I was opening greetings cards once again.

Jennifer is always full of surprises and invariably she plans something out of the ordinary for my birthday but on this occasion she was again giving nothing away so it was suggested I went to go out with a friend for the afternoon.

When we returned I was surprised to find our kitchen had been commandeered by Stephen Gill the chef from the Blue Bell Hotel in Middlesbrough, and Mark Jennisson one of the restaurant's waiters. They were in the process of preparing the most appetising meal of Salmon Roulade, Cannon of Lamb and Creme Brulee. So that was the surprise!

What an original idea, instead of going out for dinner, simply bring in the experts and have it professionally prepared for you in the comfort of your own home. I'm telling you it could catch on.

By 7.30pm several of our friends had arrived for a pink champagne reception and we spent a very convivial evening being waited on hand and foot. Many thanks are due, once again, to the general manager of the Blue Bell, Ron Darby, who along with Jennifer helped to organise such a unique dinner party.

Away from the distractions of football one of the great passions in my life is horse racing. As I've previously stated, my love of horses began at an early age when I rode my grandparents' ponies around the open fields near their Lingdale home. Later, I was fortunate to own three racehorses that were even good enough to enter the winner's enclosure on a few occasions.

My close association with horses was unexpectedly revived in February, 2001, when the mounted section of Cleveland Police ran a competition in the local schools to name their two latest equine recruits who were to patrol the Riverside Stadium on matchdays. To my surprise the names finally chosen were Mannion and Hardwick.

Having a horse named after me was quite an honour and to retain the connection with Wilf was very appropriate indeed.

The official naming of the horses, which took place at the stadium, was attended by members of Wilf's family together with some of the local school children who had suggested the names. Following the ceremony, the head of the mounted unit, Inspector Ross Sibley, told me that he felt the names were the perfect choice as we were fondly remembered Boro players of the past.

He also hoped that the horses would be part of the club for as long as Wilf and myself. I must confess that I've really become rather attached to both horses and Jennifer and I often make regular visits to the force's North Ormesby Hall stables to check on their progress.

For nearly two years in the 1950s, when I was chief coach to their national team and the country's most famous club side, PSV Eindoven, the Dutch people treated me with great kindness. Throughout the intervening years I've never lost my respect or affection for their country. Today, as we have done on many previous occasions, Jennifer and I still make regular visits to the Netherlands to stay with our dear friend Betty who lives in The Hague.

We had originally met Betty when she married a cricketing friend of mine from Middlesbrough, Barrie Allum. A draughtsman by trade, Barrie had moved to Holland with his work.

Once they were settled in their new home, we were kindly invited for a weekend break. That initial invitation evolved into a series of enjoyable holidays, which still continue even though Barrie, who was a very fit sports enthusiast, died suddenly of a heart attack a number of years ago.

Strangely, despite those frequent holidays, I'd never revisited PSV's ground since the day I left. So, in March, 2001, we decided I'd better make another sentimental journey before it became too late.

The Eindoven club, as most followers of Dutch football know, receives a massive financial investment from the Phillips Electronics Company. As no expense is spared, the club has some of the best facilities in Europe both on and off the pitch.

When we awoke on the morning of our arranged visit we were greeted by torrential rain. In fact it was so dreadful that we came very close to cancelling the two hour journey. However Betty, to her great credit, decided to brave the horrendous conditions and drove us to Eindoven.

Once we arrived at the imposing stadium we were kindly met by the club's officials who gave us a conducted tour of the ground.

As we strolled down one particular corridor in the main stand we came across, quite by chance, a photograph of yours truly. I can't begin to tell you what an immense feeling of pride welled up inside me when I saw my picture hanging on the wall. There I was alongside all the other the managers of distinction including former England boss, Bobby Robson. What a sublime moment. George Hardwick from Lingdale framed for posterity by one of the greatest clubs in European football. I was certainly glad that we'd braved the atrocious elements to make the journey.

The East Cleveland village of Lingdale has always had a very special place in my heart. After all, it was where I played my first competitive game of football for the local school team. Since those formative years, I've never forgotten my roots and have consciously always tried to retain my close ties with the area. Even to this day Jennifer and I often make frequent sentimental journeys to visit the small welcoming rural community where I spent my very happy childhood during the 1920s.

So, when I was informed that two Lingdale councillors, Steve Kay and Bruce MacKenzie, had succeeded in nominating me to receive the freedom of Redcar and Cleveland I was immensely proud. As I've highlighted before in this publication, I can think of no greater accolade than to receive what amounts to a Lifetime Achievement Award from your hometown area and I'd like to convey my sincere thanks to both Steve and Bruce for their sterling efforts.

The conferment ceremony, held on May 23, 2001, at the Redcar Bowl was a day that Jennifer and I will treasure forever. Presided over by madam mayor, Councillor Vilma Collins, it was a grand affair attended by more than 200 invited guests including my two sons Mike and Andy.

As the formal ceremony began, my nomination for the honour was publicly proposed and then seconded from the platform by Councillors Keith Pudney and Norman Davies. However, what I'd failed to appreciate was that there then follows an opportunity for anybody to object to my nomination. Happily I was spared any public embarrassment and was able to swear to uphold the Freeman's Oath.

Following my acceptance of the honour, madam mayor presented me with a handsome decorative scroll to commemorate the occasion.

The Borough's highest award was also conferred on Vera Robinson MBE a former teacher, local historian and tireless charity worker. It really puts your own achievements into perspective when you hear of people like Vera who, for more than 70 years, has devoted her whole life to constantly promoting the cultural heritage of the area. Even to this day, despite being in her late eighties, she is still an active member of the Redcar Ladies Lifeboat Guild and many other local societies and charity organisations. Vera was certainly a very worthy recipient of the Freedom of the Borough.

After the formalities were concluded, the council provided all the guests with a fine buffet lunch. However, I didn't manage to eat a great deal as I spent more than an hour signing the official programme for people to keep as a memento of such a wonderful day. As I've said before it's great to be remembered.

Well that's more or less everything up to date, and as I'm sure you'll agree the last two years have certainly been very eventful and contributed still further to what has been a rewarding life. On reflection I wouldn't change a thing.

I spent a very happy and contented childhood in Lingdale surrounded and supported by a caring family. I enjoyed to the full, all the sporting and academic opportunities, which were available to me at school. My time at Middlesbrough Football Club was the fulfilment of a youngster's dreams. To captain England and Great Britain were the pinnacles of my playing career, and thanks to my footballing ability I've made some wonderful and enduring friendships. I've also, through the game I love, been privileged to meet many famous and distinguished people from different walks of life and visited some marvellous places at home and abroad. I couldn't have asked for more.

But above all, no matter where I've been in the world, it's always reassuring to know that I can return to my roots on Teesside with its sense of community, fine coastline and beautiful surrounding countryside.

I only hope that when I do eventually "pop my clogs" and arrive outside those Pearly Gates, that God, in his infinite wisdom, takes a very close look at who it is, then hands me a new pair of football boots and says: "Go on son, go back and do it all over again."

I'd have no hesitation in carrying out the request.

George Hardwick
A Lifetime in Football

1928	Lingdale Council School
1934 - 1937	South Bank East End Juniors and Seniors
October 1935 - May 1937	Middlesbrough Amateur
May 1937 - November 1950	Middlesbrough Professional 166 appearances 7 goals
1941 - 1945	Chelsea Guest Player 75 appearances (approx, records sketchy) 2 goals
November 1950 - May 1956	Oldham Player/Manager Highest transfer fee ever paid for a full-back £15,000 Oldham Athletic Promoted 1952/53 as Third Division North Champions 190 appearances 15 goals
August 1956	US 7th Army (Stuttgart): Director of Coaching
January 1957 - June 1957	Holland: Director of Coaching & National Team Manager
August 1957 - May 1958	PSV Eindhoven: Chief Coach and Manager
August 1961 - November 1963	Middlesbrough FC: Coach to Juniors
November 1964 - May 1965	Sunderland FC: Manager
May 1968 - February 1970	Gateshead FC: Part-Time Manager

George Hardwick
Major Honours

May 1947   Captain of Great Britain

1946-1948   Captain of England

1947-1948   Captain of the Football League

1946-1950   Captain of Middlesbrough

1950-1956   Captain of Oldham Athletic

1946-1948   13 Full England Internationals

1941-1946   17 Wartime England Internationals

1947-1948   3 Football League Games

1944-1945   Wartime Southern League Cup Final winner

1952-1953   Third Division North championship medal

George Hardwick
The Representative Record

Full England International matches (13)
all as Captain

1.	28/09/46	Northern Ireland	Belfast	7-2
2.	30/09/46	Republic of Ireland	Dublin	1-0
3.	19/10/46	Wales	Maine Road	3-0
4.	27/11/46	Holland	Huddersfield	8-2
5.	12/04/47	Scotland	Wembley	1-1
6.	03/05/47	France	Highbury	3-0
7.	18/05/47	Switzerland	Zurich	0-1
8.	27/05/47	Portugal	Lisbon	10-0
9.	21/09/47	Belgium	Brussels	5-2
10.	18/10/47	Wales	Cardiff	3-0
11.	05/11/47	Northern Ireland	Goodison Park	2-2
12.	19/11/47	Sweden	Highbury	4-2
13.	10/04/48	Scotland	Glasgow	2-0

Wartime Internationals
No Caps awarded (17)
Commemorative scroll presented to players

1.	16/04/41	Wales	City Ground	4-1
2.	24/10/42	Wales	Molyneux	1-2
3.	14/04/43	Scotland	Hampden Park	4-0
4.	08/05/43	Wales	Cardiff	1-1
5.	25/09/43	Wales	Wembley	8-3

6.	16/10/43	Scotland	Manchester	8-0
7.	19/02/44	Scotland	Wembley	6-2
8.	16/09/44	Wales	Anfield	2-2
9.	14/10/44	Scotland	Wembley	6-2
10.	03/02/45	Scotland	Villa Park	3-2
11.	14/04/45	Scotland	Hampden Park	6-1
12.	05/05/45	Wales	Cardiff	3-2
13.	26/05/45	France	Wembley	2-2
14.	19/01/46	Belgium	Wembley	2-0
15.	13/04/46	Scotland	Hampden Park	0-1
16.	11/05/46	Switzerland	Chelsea	4-1
17.	19/05/46	France	Paris	1-2

Football League Games (3)
all as Captain

1.	19/02/47	Irish League	Goodison Park	4-2
2.	12/03/47	Scottish League	Glasgow	3-1
3.	17/03/48	Scottish League	Newcastle	1-1

• INDEX •